S0-CFL-870

" 'Media will take its place,' writes Hosea M. Rupprecht, FSP, in her insightful guide, *How to Watch Movies with Kids*. Parents facing the challenge of keeping media in its proper place and not at the head of the table will delight in Sr. Hosea's advice on transforming family movie time into experiences of true communication with our children. Stories, whether in books or on film, provide rich opportunities for families to engage in the nearly lost art of conversation and to share faith and values. Sr. Hosea's simple yet thoughtful strategy shows us how."

— MARY MARGARET KEATON
Author of *Imagining Faith with Kids*
(Pauline Books & Media)

"As a parent of four grown children, a Director of Faith Formation, and a VIRTUS Facilitator for the Archdiocese of Los Angeles, I have always felt that communication is the key to having an enriched and life-long relationship with our children. Sr. Hosea does a wonderful job of providing tools to help facilitate great conversations with kids when it comes to viewing and interacting with media. I especially enjoyed the stories about the saints at the end of each chapter. I will definitely recommend this book to parents at my parish with children in our religious education and RCIA-adapted for children and teens programs. I also look forward to purchasing the book for my friends who still have young children or grandchildren. Media is a gift from God and we should all be good stewards of how we can introduce, communicate, and enrich our children's lives with this gift."

— TERRI ANNE PALMER
Director Religious Education, RCIA & Faith Formation,
St. Augustine Church, Culver City, CA

"Because my husband and I are both avid movie-lovers, film-watching was a family sport when we were raising our kids. But we had no model for guiding the kids beyond our own instincts, which were not in sync. I could have used a book like Sr. Hosea Rupprecht's *How to Watch Movies with Kids*. It would have helped me analyze my instincts and clarify my own values in order to work through the differences with my husband.

"Sr. Hosea provides practical strategies for parents to help children discover the powerful impact of visual media in their own home, within the context of a loving, communicative family life. She shows how to find teachable moments without taking the fun out of family movie viewing and continues the Pauline emphasis on conversation over condemnation and collaborative viewing over strict forbidding of questionable material. All of this is set within the context of the Church's teachings on the gifts and proper usage of social communication. Armed with a set of tools for understanding how human beings construct meaning from narratives, parents can help their children form habits of media mindfulness that will last a lifetime."

— Rae Stabosz
Pauline Cooperator, Media Literacy Educator, Newark, DE

"Growing up in today's mass mediated world, our children need tools to help them develop an informed and critical understanding of the media. Sr. Hosea's book is an excellent guide for those who want to provide children with such tools. Starting with that all important notion "ask questions," Sr. Hosea develops her very effective media mindfulness strategy for the whole family. The wise use of examples and study guides takes the book up a notch beyond the offering of theoretical ideas. The entire section on producing media shows how this can be the beginning of true understanding of all media—not just movies. This is a book that will be of great use to all those who raise children and who want them to be able to respond to movies—and other media—in a critically reflective manner."

— John J. Pungente, SJ
Director, Jesuit Communication Project, Toronto, Ontario

"How to Watch Movies with Kids is a practical guide for parents or beginning catechists to prime children to become critical and discerning film viewers. As a means of contemporary storytelling, films communicate meaning and values that may affirm or oppose our primary family values. Sr. Rupprecht imparts uncomplicated steps for engaging in critical reflection, and dialogue for unpacking the meaning and message of a film by resourcefully offering strategies that can definitely be adapted to any context. The author crafts a solid foundation and guidelines for parents and catechists to be able to enhance the quality and depth of their communication through the use of contemporary films."

— SR. ANGELA ANN ZUKOWSKI, MHSH, D.MIN.
Professor, Department of Religious Studies, University of Dayton

HOW TO WATCH MOVIES WITH KIDS

HOW TO WATCH MOVIES WITH KIDS

A Values-Based Strategy

Hosea M. Rupprecht, FSP

auline

BOOKS & MEDIA

Boston

Library of Congress Cataloging-in-Publication Data

Rupprecht, Hosea M.

How to watch movies with kids : a values-based strategy / Hosea M. Rupprecht.

p. cm.

Includes bibliographical references and webliography.

ISBN 0-8198-3398-3 (pbk.)

1. Motion pictures and children. 2. Motion pictures--Moral and ethical aspects. 3. Children's films--Catalogs. I. Title.

PN1995.9.C45R87 2011

791.43083--dc22

2010049377

Many manufacturers and sellers distinguish their products through the use of trademarks. Any trademarked designations that appear in this book are used by permission or in good faith.

The Scripture quotations contained herein are from the *New Revised Standard Version Bible: Catholic Edition,* copyright © 1989, 1993, Division of Christian Education of the National Council of the Churches of Christ in the United States of America. Used by permission. All rights reserved.

Excerpts from the English translation of the *Catechism of the Catholic Church* for use in the United States of America, copyright © 1994, United States Catholic Conference, Inc.—Libreria Editrice Vaticana. Used with permission.

Cover design by Rosana Usselmann

Cover art and interior art by Chris Ware

All rights reserved. No part of this book may be reproduced or transmitted in any form or by any means, electronic or mechanical, including photocopying, recording, or by any information storage and retrieval system, without permission in writing from the publisher.

"P" and PAULINE are registered trademarks of the Daughters of St. Paul.

Copyright © 2011, Daughters of St. Paul

Published by Pauline Books & Media, 50 Saint Pauls Avenue, Boston, MA 02130-3491

Printed in the U.S.A.

www.pauline.org

Pauline Books & Media is the publishing house of the Daughters of St. Paul, an international congregation of women religious serving the Church with the communications media.

1 2 3 4 5 6 7 8 9   15 14 13 12 11

To Sr. Marie Paul Curley, FSP,
for your encouragement and support.

To my mentor and colleague,
Sr. Rose Pacatte, FSP, in gratitude.

And to my sister, Jacinta,
fellow movie lover and confidante.
Love you, sis.

Contents

Introduction

"C'mon, Mom, everyone's seeing it," your child says to you. The latest movie is out in the theater, and though other parents are taking their kids, you're not quite sure if you should take yours. The kids have seen the billboards along the road, the advertisements on TV, and know the characters from the toys in their last fast-food meal. They have heard other kids talking about the movie—and so, says your little one, why can't I go see it?

What do you do? What is your strategy when it comes to your children and their media consumption?

Catholic parents (or anyone raising kids these days) have their jobs cut out for them when it comes to media. The church calls media "gifts of God," but the messages presented by the media do not always agree with our core values of love of God and love of neighbor. As a parent, you not only want to pass on to your children good values but also the faith and morals that you believe in. Sometimes the media can help, other times it presents a challenge.

I was nine years old the first time I ventured into a movie theater. The film was *Star Wars* (which we now call *Star Wars Episode IV: A*

New Hope). I watched it over and over on video during many hours of babysitting in the years that followed. Thus began my friendship with movies and the stories they tell. It is a relationship that has endured to this day, but it had a rocky start. I didn't often have the opportunity to see the films I wanted to see, those that other kids I knew were seeing. Instead, my film fare was old westerns, swashbucklers (*The Adventures of Robin Hood* with Errol Flynn and Olivia de Havilland being my favorite), and Humphrey Bogart. Eventually, the desire to see movies that were made in the decade in which I lived grew too strong and I took matters into my own hands.

I began watching movies at the homes of my friends. That's where I saw *Raiders of the Lost Ark* and *Star Trek II: The Wrath of Khan*. I definitely felt guilty, but I was not penitent. I enjoyed the experience of watching movies with my peers, being able to relate to my friends outside of school, and to talk about what we liked and didn't like about the movies. I enjoyed the movies themselves—the humor, relationships, and details of the stories. I now had some movies in common with my friends, and I wasn't the weird kid anymore. I'm not saying sneaking away to see movies was the right thing to do, but since I didn't understand why I couldn't see certain movies, at the time it seemed like my best option.

The media strategy I grew up on was *you're not allowed*. No explanation, no motivation to help me understand why I wasn't allowed. I just wasn't.

Times and parenting methods have changed since the 1970s. The "just say no" strategy is no longer encouraged for twenty-first-century kids. Kids today want to know why their parents make the decisions they do, especially if they have potentially embarrassing consequences for them in relation to their peers. There was a lot of media around when I was growing up, but kids today are born into a world saturated with media. Entertainment through TV, movies, MP3 players, the Internet, and gaming have, to some degree, taken the place of playing catch, jump rope, and hide and seek. Because media is so prevalent, it is important for children to develop the critical thinking and communication skills they need in order to navigate this media world and grow into discerning media users. In this book, I offer a strategy for Catholic parents (or anyone who is raising children) that can help them communicate with their children about information and entertainment media from an early age.

Why Movies? They're Stories!

We all like to hear stories. When the Campfire Girls troop I belonged to as a child went on weekend campouts, we would sit around the campfire at night and tell spooky stories trying to scare one another! The kids I babysat as a teenager liked to have the same story read to them over and over again. Stories have the ability to draw us into the experiences of the characters as if they were our own. We feel with them because they say something to us of what it means to be human (even if the characters themselves are not human).

When Jesus spoke to the people of his day, he told stories and gave them endings that his audience did not expect. They held a bit of a shock value and made people think about what the story could mean for them. With these stories he not only held people spellbound but was able to impart his teaching in an entertaining way. Remember the parable of the Good Samaritan (Lk 10:25–37)? In answer to a question from a lawyer, Jesus begins teaching about loving one's neighbor. But the lawyer, probably feeling a bit uncomfortable with the answer, wants to make sure he understands correctly. He asks for clarification.

Jesus expands by telling a story. A traveler gets beaten up on the road and left for dead. A couple of people, whom you think would show compassion, instead pass him by. The least expected helper, the foreigner, the outcast, is the one who does what is right. By putting the teaching in the context of a story with good guys, bad guys, plot, a bit of action, and an unexpected twist, Jesus got his point across and challenged the lawyer to "Go and do likewise" (Lk 10:37).

Movies can be modern-day parables. They all have some point of view or way of looking at the world that undergirds the story. It might take a little digging (and sometimes a second viewing) to understand what viewpoint a movie is trying to get across. To complicate matters, you may find that your opinion about the movie differs from those of others. A movie might present a story that has values you as a believer can embrace, such as compassion or redemption. It could also present values inconsistent with yours, such as revenge or violence. Just to keep things interesting, most movies will have elements of both.

That being said, how do you make sense of the messages presented in a movie? How do you help your children make sense of it all? Where to begin? I hope that the following chapters will give you ideas on how to sharpen your own skills when it comes to critical thinking about movies and give you suggestions on how to introduce critical thinking to your little ones. Very young children don't yet have the ability to analyze the subtleties of movie messages. They can, however, ask questions and answer the ones you ask them. You are the one who, by modeling it yourself, can provide for your child the tools they will need to ask meaningful questions about the movies they experience. As they grow older, the questions being asked of the movies can turn into many conversations and teachable moments about all kinds of things: values, what's right and wrong, and who we are as human persons and children of God. By laying a foundation where conversation as a family is encouraged, you will teach your children that they can talk to you, not only about movies, but about anything and everything—whatever is going on in their lives.

Why Build a Media Strategy?

"Watch movies with my kids and talk about them. That doesn't sound too hard. Why do I need a strategy?"

Well, why not? As parents, you probably have strategies or plans for who gets up when the baby cries at night, how to potty train the toddler, how to make sure the kids get good nutrition, saving up for their college funds, and making sure they know how much they are loved by you and by God. You may have even received advice from your own parents, other family members, pediatricians, or parenting books about how to go about these tasks. Why not about the media? Among the many influences in your children's lives, like you and God, media will claim its place. A strategy for teaching your children to ask questions of the media in light of their faith and its values will help you help them grow into people who use their faith and values as a basis for making good media choices.

What to Expect

This book has your needs and expectations in mind as you raise children in a world quite different from your own childhood experience. Your kids are learning right from wrong, being introduced to values and morals first by observation (especially watching you!) and, when they start school, learning from their teachers and peers. It is during the formative years that they take the first steps to developing moral awareness and letting it guide their actions. Whether your kids are older or younger, developing and growing in the ability to communicate values and question media is appropriate.

The chapters in this book are meant to build one on top of another. If you would like a peek at what the end-result of the book will be—a family media strategy—skip ahead to Chapter Five and glance at the questions that make up the strategy. However, these will make a lot more sense when read along with what comes before. Chapter One introduces you to the media age and the joys and challenges of raising kids in this media-saturated culture. Chapter Two focuses on values: what they are, why they're important, and how they can be a great starting point for introducing children to the art of questioning the media. Chapter Three opens up the world of movie making. Plot, character, and film techniques will help you understand better what goes into a movie story. Chapter Four will take you to the next step of making meaning from movies. Discover the difference between content and context. Learn what kind of questions can be asked of the movie. Knowing what genre a movie belongs to, for example, gives you clues into how it will make meaning. Chapter Six suggests some media-related fun activities for the whole family. Finally, Chapter Seven will provide you with some resources to aid in carrying out your strategy, such as film guides, a list of themes and movies, and helpful Web sites and books. One thing to remember: although this book will focus on the medium of film, what is said about movies also applies to other kinds of media, such as print media, television, Internet, and gaming (to name just a few).

Saints to Guide Us

What a gift we Catholics have in the saints! These people who have lived virtuous and faithful lives, sometimes amid great difficulty and suffering, give us an example of how to live Christ-like lives in our own day and age. The saints can be guides for us in our life journeys, not only through their example, but through prayer and the support that the communion of saints affords us who still await our seat at the heavenly banquet.

Stories about the lives of the saints were abundant in the home of my childhood. I read a lot of them in book form and others I saw on film, *The Song of Bernadette* being the one I remember best. Because saints are such an integral part of our Catholic tradition, each of the first five chapters of the book will end with the story of a saint or blessed of the Church. This person can be a guide as you explore the information presented in the chapter and work to build your family's media strategy.

There's a song by the Christian group Phillips, Craig & Dean called *I Want to Be Just Like You.*[1] The lyrics of the chorus are: "Lord, I want to be just like you, 'cause he wants to be just like me. I want to be a holy example for his innocent eyes to see. Help me be a living Bible, Lord, that my little boy can read. I want to be just like you 'cause he wants to be like me." So is expressed a father's desire to be a good example to his child. As a Catholic parent, your desire is the same. May our Lord, his blessed Mother, and the saints be with you on this journey.

---

1. Copyright © 1994 Dawn Treader Music (SESAC) (adm. at EMICMGPublishing. com) / Praise Song Press (ASCAP). All rights reserved. Used by permission.

Chapter One

Raising Children in a Media Age

Total Access Pass

Think back to when you were a kid. How much access to media did you have? Radio? Television? Movies? Video games? When I was growing up, the video game console and home computers were just beginning to make the circuit. I played Atari video games and was an expert at Space Invaders! Our home computer, a Commodore 64, making its debut in 1982, was a best-seller while it was around.

Now think about your kids' media access. What a difference, right? Kids today have almost instant access to media in so many forms right from the moment they enter the world. When your child was born, was there a family member capturing the moment on video or clicking away with a digital camera? If not in the delivery room, probably fairly soon afterward! The baby of a long-time family friend of mine was born prematurely and spent months in the hospital. During that time she kept everyone updated on her little boy's progress via a blog. People were able to leave comments offering prayers of support and hope. What a wonderful service media can provide!

Media is everywhere. You cannot get around it. Media messages come in many forms: song lyrics, magazine articles, information obtained via the Internet, TV shows, video games, movies, advertisements, instant messaging, and many others. Media is a force to be reckoned with, and as a Catholic parent in this media age, it is something you cannot ignore. Just by being born in this era, your child has a "total access pass" to the media that surrounds her. Once she gets to the age where experiencing media becomes an everyday occurrence, she will need your help to understand the messages she's getting from the media world.

A while back there was a television advertisement for Windows operating system. In it a little girl named Kylie took a picture of her

fish with a digital camera, downloaded it to the computer, enhanced the photo, and emailed it to her parents. The tagline was, "I'm a PC and I'm four and a half."

With this kind of access, kids need the guidance of parents not only in making sense out of the messages they receive, but also in balancing their time between media and other activities such as sports, playtime with friends, or school work. Media experiences are fun for kids, but limits set by you provide the balance they need. Developing your family strategy will help.

Communication

Communication is an essential parenting skill. If you communicate about anything and everything with your kids, they will be more likely to communicate with you about everything. Talking about the seemingly insignificant things in life will give them the practice and permission to talk about the

One media-related concern parents today have to deal with is the safety of their children on the Internet. The Church is very aware of the need to protect children, especially after the sufferings of the past decade regarding sexual abuse of children by clergy and others in positions of trust. The National Catholic Risk Retention Group, Inc. is dedicated to doing everything possible to help keep children safe. To this end they have instituted Virtus programs, designed to educate people about detecting the signs of abuse and best practice standards for preventing or responding to possible abuse. Many topics are covered in the programs and information available on their Web site: www.virtus.org, including Internet safety for kids. Many parishes now require Virtus training for volunteers or ministers working with children in any way. You may be interested in checking it out.

really important aspects of life. Communicating about media is included. Being able to enter into conversation about media experiences with kids lets them know it's okay to talk about them. You send the message that you want to be open with them about your thoughts and, more importantly, that you want to know *their* thoughts about the media they experience.

When I was manager of one of our Pauline Books & Media Centers, Tess, an employee, would tell me what was going on with her daughter, Kate. I knew Kate personally from the volunteer work she did at the bookstore. I was always impressed at her level of maturity for her age. I remember once telling Tess, "You are doing such a wonderful job with Kate. What's your secret?" She answered, "I don't treat her like a kid, and we talk about everything; we always have."

Communicating about media can be a challenge for parents of older children because they don't want to be interrupted during their favorite TV show or film. But if you start when they're young, communication becomes natural. There was an interesting study done in 2005 in this regard.[1] The researchers studied parental interaction with preschoolers as they watched TV together. A program was broadcast with a "Mommy Bar," a line of scrolling text at the bottom that had information for the parent such as recipes, jokes, etc. The researchers wondered if an educationally enhanced Mommy Bar would increase parent-child interaction. The text at the bottom was changed to give parents suggested ways to comment on the program for the child, such as "Does your room ever get messy?", "Why is she sad?", or "Was that a good thing to do?" They found that the educationally enhanced bar significantly increased parent-child interaction. Parents were better able to help kids connect what was on the screen to their lives.

Think about it this way. You are reading a storybook to your child. Do you just read the words on the page? You explore the story with

---

1. Anna Akerman, Shalom M. Fisch, et al., "Coviewing Preschool Television in the US: Eliciting Parent-Child Interaction Via On Screen Prompts," *Journal of Children and Media* 2, no. 2 (July 2008): 163–173.

her. You label things: "Look at the clouds." You ask questions: "What color is that ball?" You connect with life: "They're eating ice cream. You like ice cream. What's your favorite flavor?" You can do the exact same thing when experiencing media with your children. If they learn the skills needed at an early age, they will begin communicating with the media of their own accord as they grow older.

Passing on Values and Beliefs

The Catholic Church has always taught that parents are the primary educators of their children. When a child is baptized, the parents are reminded of their obligation to pass the faith on to the child. This is not seen as a burdensome task, but rather as a privilege. The little one you hold in your arms at his Baptism will need to learn about how much he is loved by God, how to follow the life God wishes for him, and how to live the human and Gospel values demonstrated by Jesus. But how?

I learned the basics of the faith from a question and answer catechism. It asked questions, and I memorized the answers. I was drilled to make sure I had the answers right. Having a pretty good memory, that wasn't too hard for me. I could list off the seven sacraments, recite my Acts of Faith, Hope, and Love, and Act of Contrition by heart, and knew the Spiritual and Corporal Works of Mercy, plus everything else that marked me as a practicing Catholic. I was a good kid, being taught what was right from wrong. I was rewarded when I did things right and punished when I did things wrong. Living the faith was black and white. Either I knew the answers or I didn't.

It was not until much later in life, after I entered the convent, that I began to realize that just knowing the answers was not good enough. The faith is not question and answer but a relationship with the God of love. I learned that things are not always black and white, but that living the faith sometimes involves conversations with other people, learning from what another thinks. Lived faith needs a firmer foundation than just questions and answers.

When you think and pray about how to best pass the faith on to your children, please take this into consideration. Yes, it is important to memorize the prayers, the sacraments, and the responses for Sunday Eucharist. But it is even more important to be for your children a living example of what a vibrant relationship with God looks like. It is easy to understand the "what" of the Catholic faith. It is harder to understand the "why." Knowing why we believe what we believe and do what we do, and the One who enables us to do it, is key to then being able to teach another to "go and do likewise" (Lk 10:37).

Developing Lasting Relationships

At this point, maybe you have a question in your mind. "What is the underlying purpose of all this talk regarding communicating about the media?" The goal is to develop lasting relationships with your children. Communication with children when they are young can help to develop a pattern that could result in lasting relationships. My friend, Tess, and her daughter have this kind of relationship, built over years of communicating with one another. Kate is now going to college, and she still talks to her mother about all that is going on in her life.

"Control is for the moment. Communication lasts a lifetime." This phrase was coined by my colleague, Sr. Rose Pacatte. Think of it this way: *how* you teach is *what* you teach. The attitude with which you go about teaching your children about faith, life, and values will be the attitude they will pick up. Communication is one of those abilities that will turn into a life skill if they learn it from you. When children are very young there is definitely a place for control. In fact, the American Academy of Pediatrics (AAP) discourages exposure to screen media for children under the age of two.[2] But even then that doesn't mean there is no communication. The same AAP report also encourages families to view and discuss television programs together.

I've watched a fair share of ABC's *Supernanny* on TV. I think what first drew me to the show was just how horribly undisciplined some of the kids were. Some of the things that I saw on the show would never have happened in the home of my childhood! I felt bad for the parents. Some of them just needed some help gaining perspective or learning new skills. After watching the program for a while, I realized that Supernanny (Jo Frost) has a consistent technique for "time outs." She calls it the "naughty step technique."[3] When the child misbehaves, she first gets a warning that her behavior is unacceptable, and, if she repeats the behavior, she will be put on the naughty step (or chair, or corner). The parent's voice should be calm, not angry, and have a low, authoritative tone. When she misbehaves again, she gets put on the step immediately. The parent explains *why* she is there and how long she must stay (one minute for each year of age). If the child tries to get away, return her with gentle but firm movements and keep on doing this as long as it takes. Once she has done her time, the parent crouches down to her level and explains again, in a low, authoritative voice why she was put there and then asks for an apology. Once she apologizes, she's smothered with hugs, kisses, and affirmations from the parent.

I found this methodology a refreshing example of the power of positive communication. When a parent says no to something, be it a snack before dinner, a TV show, or a movie, it is paramount that the motivation be explained. This communicates to your children the

---

2. American Academy of Pediatrics Committee on Public Education, "Children, Adolescents, and Television," *Pediatrics* 107 (2001): 424. This can be found online at: www.pediatrics.org/cgi/content/full/107/2/423.

3. Supernanny Team, "The Naughty Step Technique," October 26, 2006, www.supernanny.com/Advice/-/supernanny-techniques/-/Discipline-and-reward/The-naughty-step-technique.aspx.

reason for your choice, the "why" they need in order to understand. Otherwise, "just saying no" is too black and white. It offers no room for communication and teaches nothing except resentment and control. Communication, on the other hand, opens up so many potentially teachable moments between parent and child that the possibilities are endless.

For example, your son, Kevin, six years old, hears about the latest animated film from television commercials and billboards. He sees funny creatures and talking aliens. What little boy wouldn't be attracted by funny creatures and talking aliens? He asks you if he can go see the movie. You have a few options for how you respond.

Option One

Parent: "No, Kevin, you can't go."

Kevin: "But why not?"

Parent: "Because I said so," or "Because you're too young."

Option Two

Parent: "What's it about?"

Kevin: "Funny creatures and talking aliens. It looks fun."

Parent: "I tell you what. I'll look at some reviews, talk to your [other parent], and then we'll decide. How's that?"

Kevin: "Okay."

If you consider these two options, you see that option one leaves no room for communication. This is an example of control, not communication. Option two, on the other hand, is wide open with communication possibilities. The parent has not yet committed to a course of action, but dialogue has taken place. This shows respect on the parent's part toward the child, and the child toward the parent. The conversation might continue in these ways:

New Release!

BOOKS & MEDIA

50 St. Paul's Avenue   Boston, MA 02130

617-522-8911

Orders: 800-876-4463 FAX 617-524-8035

www.pauline.org

After deciding yes, you tell Kevin, "Okay, Kevin. We read some reviews, and it looks good, so we'll go see the movie with [other parent] on Saturday, but remember our family movie strategy? We'll talk about what you thought of the movie when we come home!"

Kevin: "Cool! Thanks."

Or if you decide no, your continued dialogue may sound like this: "Kevin, your [other parent] and I read some reviews and talked about it. It looks like this movie might be a bit too scary for you. They didn't show that part on the TV commercial. The nightmares you have are never fun, are they? We don't want you to get nightmares because of this. We love you too much. So maybe when you get older we could rent the DVD and see it then."

Kevin: "Okay, but the other kids at school will think I'm a scaredy-cat if I don't see it."

Parent: "Don't you worry about them. You know you're not a scaredy-cat, and I know you're not a scaredy-cat, so it really doesn't matter what they say. We said no because we love you and don't want you to have nightmares. Okay?"

Kevin: "Alright."

Parent: "How about we go to the playground on Saturday and play catch instead?"

Kevin: "Sounds great!"

From these examples, you can see that by asking questions and giving answers that explain the parent's reasons for their answers, parent and child entered into a meaningful conversation. And no matter which way the parent decides to go, communication happened.

As your children get older, giving the reasons behind your decisions will become extremely important for your relationship with them. Trust, an important part of any relationship, will grow between you and your child. By providing reasons, you teach your child to give reasons in return (how you teach is what you teach!).

Communicating with your children about their media choices is one way to develop a bond of trust between you and them. When your kids are small, it seems like you will have them forever. When it's time to let them go off into their own lives, the quality of your ongoing relationship will depend in large part on the level of communication and trust you have had with them as they grew up. Trust is key to a lasting relationship.

What the Church Says

"With great power comes great responsibility." This quote from the 2002 movie, *Spider-Man*, could also be said to those who produce media. The enormous influence of the media in our society is something the Church has concerned itself with since the early part of the twentieth century.

The first documents,[4] although heavy with warnings for people to protect themselves from morally bad films, acknowledged that the media are "gifts of God," invented by human ingenuity, itself a gift from a loving God.[5] They acknowledge the contributions media make to society as sources of information, entertainment, and education while encouraging Catholic participation in producing media.

Vatican II's Decree on the Means of Social Communication, *Inter Mirifica*, continued the trend by encouraging media consumers, especially young people, to be critical thinkers and to talk about media in order to understand its messages.[6] It called for responsibility on the part of media makers to respect the dignity of the human person and to promote human and Gospel values.

In order to continue to provide Church guidance in the ever-changing field of media, *Inter Mirifica* asked that a special Vatican office be

---

4. *Vigilante Cura* (1939) and *Miranda Prorsus* (1957).
5. Pius XII, *Miranda Prorsus: Motion Pictures, Radio, and Television*, 1.
6. *Inter Mirifica*, 10.

set up. Today this office is known as the Pontifical Council for Social Communications and since Vatican II it has released seven documents on various aspects of the media (see sidebar).

The popes have also commented on the media in a variety of forums. Pope John Paul II's last apostolic letter was about the media: *The Rapid Development* (January 2005). It called the Church's attention to the culture created by communications media and reminded us that "a *vast work of formation* is needed to assure that the mass media be known and used intelligently and appropriately."[7] Yearly, the World Day of Communications gives the Holy Father an opportunity to comment on various aspects of media. In the address for 2007, Pope Benedict XVI said this regarding children and the media:

The relationship of children, media, and education can be considered from two perspectives: the formation of children by the media; and the formation of children to respond appropriately to the media. A kind

Major Church Documents on the Media

○ *Vigilante Cura,* Pope Pius XI, 1936

○ *Miranda Prorsus,* Pope Pius XII, 1957

○ *Inter Mirifica,* Vatican II, 1963

○ *Communio et Progressio,* Pontifical Commission for the Means of Social Communication, 1971

○ *Aetatis Novae,* Pontifical Council for Social Communication, 1992

○ *The Rapid Development,* John Paul II, 2005 (his last official document)

○ From 1967 to present, Pontifical Messages for World Communications Day All available on the Vatican's Web site: www.vatican.va

Other Documents of the Pontifical Council for Social Communication

○ Pornography and Violence, 1989

○ Ethics in Advertising, 1997

○ Ethics in Communication, 2000

○ Ethics and the Internet, 2002

○ The Church and the Internet, 2002

---

7. John Paul II, *The Rapid Development,* 11.

of reciprocity emerges which points to the responsibilities of the media as an industry and to the need for active and critical participation of readers, viewers, and listeners. Within this framework, training in the proper use of media is essential for the cultural, moral, and spiritual development of children.

SAINTS TO GUIDE US
Saint Gianna Molla

In her own day, as a mother raising three young children, Saint Gianna had her share of challenges, just as you do today.

Saint Gianna is a patron saint of mothers, together with Saint Ann and Saint Monica. She also shares her profession with Saint Luke, patron saint of doctors. She is best known for the heroic act of self-sacrifice that resulted in her death at age thirty-nine. A fibroid (benign tumor of the uterus) was discovered when she was two months pregnant with her fourth child. After weighing all her options, and ruling out an abortion or a hysterectomy, she decided on the path that would be the safest for her unborn child. As a medical doctor, she knew that there were serious risks involved and that the pregnancy would be difficult. For this reason she made it clear that if there was danger of death, the baby's life was to have preference. The surgery to remove the tumor was successful, and she gave birth to a healthy baby girl, Gianna Emanuela. However, Gianna continued to suffer greatly and a severe infection (septic peritonitis) caused her death seven days later, April 28, 1962. She was canonized by Pope John Paul II on May 16, 2004. Gianna's husband, ninety-one-year-old Pietro Molla, her three surviving children, her granddaughter, surviving siblings, former patients, and many friends were in attendance at the ceremony.

Gianna was the tenth of thirteen children, born on October 4, 1922, to Maria and Albert Beretta. Gianna's faith and sense of service to others was nurtured in her family life. In the Beretta family, each day began with Mass and ended with the Rosary. The Beretta's raised their children to be satisfied with what they had, to give to others, to pray authentically, and to live lives of Christian service.

At age fifteen, Gianna attended her school's weekend retreat. It became a turning point in her spiritual life. At this time, she began to discern her path in life. After high school she began studying medicine, intending to become a medical missionary. The death of her parents and the hardships of World War II made medical school a challenge, but she graduated with honors and pursued a specialization in pediatrics.

Pietro Molla lived across the street from Gianna's office. He began to take notice of Dr. Beretta, and they soon grew close. Pietro and Gianna were married by her own brother, Father Guiseppe Beretta, on September 24, 1955. As an engineer, Pietro's work often took him far from home. The letters between the two bear witness to their deep love for God, for each other, and for their children, Pierluigi, Maria Zita (Mariolina), and Laura.

With Pietro often away on business trips, Gianna's life was intense as she handled her many responsibilities as wife, mother, and doctor. The strength of her faith and the conviction that her life was to be spent for others gave her the help she needed. Gianna paid special attention to raising her children to be people of faith, loving God, praying, and remembering to make their examination of conscience every night, asking God for forgiveness.

Gianna Molla is a wonderful example of a Christian working mother. Her holiness, her dedication to her patients, both in body and soul, her love of her husband and children, and the sacrifice she made, choosing the life of her child over her own, makes her a holy model and inspiration for wives and mothers today. Saint Gianna Molla, pray for us.

QUESTIONS FOR FAMILY CONVERSATION

1. What media is present in your home? How many TVs, radios, CD or portable music players, and computers are in the house? What about cell phones? What kind of access do your kids have to them? Where is the technology? Is it in a place where supervision is possible? What is the purpose of media in your family?

2. Parents: What is your attitude toward communication with your children? Do you encourage them to talk to you? When they speak, do you give them your attention?

3. Kids: Do you feel loved when you talk with your parents about things? Are there things you are afraid to tell your parents? Why? Talk together about those things and why it is good to talk about them. Do you feel able to ask your parents questions?

4. Parents and kids: Think of one way that you can grow in your relationships with each other. Then focus on trying it out for a determined time, like a week or a month.

5. How does the Church teaching that "media are gifts of God" make you feel? Talk about those feelings with other family members. Do you agree? Why or why not? If you have some time, choose one of the documents from the list on page 19 and then talk with the family about any new insights you gained into the media.

Chapter Two

The Starting Point: Values Articulation

Importance of Values

Do you remember when you learned how to ride a bike? The fun and the thrill? Maybe you haven't ridden a bike for a long time, but you would still be able to do it if the opportunity presented itself. There are things in life that once learned can never really be unlearned, things like riding a bike, swimming, or playing a musical instrument. If you don't do it for a while, a little practice gets you right back on track. It's the same with values. Once learned they can't be unlearned. If they are not practiced regularly, their effectiveness in your life can wane, but you will always know what they are and how to live them. Making the effort to keep practicing our values is the work of living a life in imitation of Jesus Christ.

Values are ideas or ideals that give direction and purpose to our life. They are not something we learn out of a book. Children learn values first by observing them being lived by other people, most of all, you, their parents. When you take your child into your arms and tell her that you love her, she knows instinctively that it is true. She can feel it. She can't define love (who can?) but she can say, "Love is when Mommy and Daddy hug me tight."

When you were little, you learned values from your family. Now it's your turn to live those values to the best of your ability so that your kids will pick them up. As manager of a Catholic bookstore, I had the pleasure of talking to lots of young parents. Most of the time, they were looking for material on the basics of the Catholic Faith. They had learned these basics when they were children, and even though some of them still went to Mass every Sunday, they had not brought their understanding of the faith to an adult level. Now they had young children who were asking questions about God, church, morality, and everything else under the sun. They considered themselves ill-equipped to answer some questions and were taking steps to understand better so that they could, in turn, explain the faith to their kids.

I think it's much the same when it comes to values. You learn them as children and live them as you grow up, sometimes well and sometimes not so well. But when your kids come along wondering why you do what you do, it's not easy to articulate clearly, in a way they can under-

stand, the why of your actions. Ultimately, we all do what we do because of our values. Why do you or your spouse (or both) go to work every day? In order to support your family. Why do you nurture your children? Because you love them. Why do you teach them to be kind to other kids? Because you are caring and want them to be caring also.

What I am describing here are human and Gospel values. Just like faith builds on reason, Gospel values build on human values. Human values are universal. They apply to everyone by virtue of being human. These values contribute to the character development of your child. Values such as honesty, courage, justice, respect, tolerance, kindness, solidarity, and empathy are the foundations of character. Your children's characters will develop as they make a habit of doing the right thing, acting on the human values they have instinctively. You have shown them what it looks like to live them.

Another way of looking at character is what you do when no one is watching. A person who truly lives out of their values will do what is right because it is right and not because someone else is watching. This is what you aim to do as a thoughtful Christian trying to live as best you can each day. Of course, God sees our every thought and action. "Nothing is covered up that will not be uncovered, and nothing secret that will not become known. Therefore whatever you have said in the dark will be heard in the light" (Lk 12:2–3a). This is not cause for fear but rejoicing, for the Father who sees in secret will reward you (cf. Mt 6:4).

Gospel values build upon human ones. Kindness is still kindness but motivated by the example of Jesus. Love is lifted to a whole new level in the light of Jesus's sacrifice on the cross. Peacemaking gives us "children of God" status. The beatitudes in Matthew's Gospel (5:1–12) are the clearest articulation of Gospel values. Other Gospel values are found in the parables of Jesus, such as forgiveness in the story of the Prodigal Son and charity in the story of the Good Samaritan.

Even more are the values gleaned from the stories about Jesus himself, his own actions, forgiving the sinful woman, healing the blind man, blessing the children, feeding the multitudes, and giving himself in the Eucharist.

If you are anything like me, you struggle day in and day out with the values presented by Jesus. But that does not mean you stop trying. Being able to admit to your children that you don't always live out your values and need to ask God's forgiveness gives them the assurance they need to know that even if they go astray, you (and God) will always welcome them back into your loving arms.

Empathy: An Essential Value for Kids

Values take time to develop in a child's life. He's not going to get it overnight. Why should he be nice to someone who is not being nice to him? It's difficult for a child to understand. By helping your child develop a sense of empathy, all the other values will fall into place a little easier. Empathy means a person can feel what another person feels without actually having to go through the same experience. Asking a child, "How would you feel if that happened to you?" can lead to many conversations about the important things in life, the values exemplified by Jesus.

Children can begin showing signs of empathy around age three.[1] If your child sees you are disturbed about something, she may try to comfort you. What children are unable to do at this point is exercise the compassion that is a response to feelings of empathy. That comes later, once they have developed a sense of self-awareness and the beginnings of conscience. That does not mean that you can't start

---

1. Cf. Dr. Charles E. Schaefer and Theresa Foy Digeronimo, *Ages and Stages: A Parent's Guide to Normal Childhood Development* (New York: John Wiley & Sons, Inc., 2000), 100–101.

planting seeds. But be patient! Kids learn lessons very slowly through plenty of repetition.

The ability to feel empathy is intrinsic to human nature. By virtue of being human, our hearts are programmed to empathize with another person. But that does not mean you don't have to work at it yourself and foster it in your children. Talking about feelings and helping children to identify feelings is a good way to foster the growth of empathy.

Empathy enables you to "walk in another's shoes," to experience life from another's point of view. In the classic film, *To Kill a Mockingbird*, Atticus tells Scout that you can't understand another person "until you climb into his skin and walk around in it." This is empathy. Learning how to see something from another person's perspective is essential to character development and formation of conscience. In opposition to empathy is unbridled selfishness, always focused on oneself rather than on other people. If I can only see a situation from my own point of view, I cannot understand the other's feelings. I cannot see their perspective. I am closed to what the other has to say. I do not respect that person if I cannot at least be open to their thoughts on a situation. If I cannot empathize, I will be stuck in my own little world, fearful and arrogant. Meaningful relationships will not be possible because a relationship goes two ways.

On the other hand, if I can empathize, then I will not only understand other people's feelings and see things from their perspective, but I can be kind, caring, forgiving, and compassionate. I can find the same shortcomings and fears in myself that I can see in others. If I can empathize, relationships can be established and grow.

Values and Catholic Living

Fostering a life lived on the foundation of human and Gospel values is where the teachings of Jesus and Holy Mother Church meet everyday life. The "where the rubber meets the road" cliché applies here. Very few people's lives are oriented by one defining moment. Most people respond to God's invitation to holiness by making small choices day in and day out to act in a manner pleasing to God. When you miss the mark, you ask God's forgiveness and try again. In my own life, when I avail myself of the Sacrament of Reconciliation, I find that I often go before God with the same small, petty things time and time again. With the grace of the sacrament, we try again to make choices according to our values.

The why and how of living a moral life represent a big chunk of Church teaching. One of the four pillars of the *Catechism of the Catholic Church* is the moral life, entitled "Life in Christ." Where I have used the word *values*, the *Catechism* uses the word *virtues*. "A virtue is a habitual and firm disposition to do the good. It allows the person not only to perform good acts, but to give the best of himself. The virtuous person tends toward the good with all his sensory and spiritual powers, he pursues the good and chooses it in concrete actions" (no. 1803).

This is great in theory, but you know as well as I do that in practice things can be very different. Enter the moral imagination. Vigen Guroian, a professor of theology and ethics at Loyola College in Baltimore, defines moral imagination as "the very process by which the self makes metaphors out of images given by experience and then employs these metaphors to find and suppose moral correspondences in experience."[2] In other words, if we reflect and process our experiences, taking to heart what we learn from them, they will help us when it comes to making decisions in new circumstances.

The *Catechism of the Catholic Church* says the education of conscience is a lifelong task. "From the earliest years, it awakens the

---

2. Vigen Guroian, "Awakening the Moral Imagination: Teaching Virtues Through Fairy Tales," *The Intercollegiate Review* (Fall 1996), www.mmisi.org/ir/32_01/guroian.pdf.

child to the knowledge and practice of the interior law recognized by conscience. Prudent education teaches virtue" (no. 1784). The moral imagination is one tool of formation of conscience. It takes what you experience, helps you process it, and adds what is learned to the store of understanding upon which you draw when making concrete choices. The way your children experience media and make meaning of it contributes to the formation of their consciences through the process of moral imagination.

Your moral imagination has been active since you were a little child. You've been forming your conscience for years now. Conscience and values are so close to the core of who you are as a follower of Christ, acting on them is mostly automatic. When you decide to be kind to your neighbor by giving her a cup of sugar, you don't consciously think it through; you just do it because you're a nice person (and have enough sugar to share). You've learned the values of sharing, caring, and kindness and act on them instinctively, without a long thought process.

Still, it's good to stop every once in a while and spend some thoughtful time considering your values. When I give workshops, I ask participants to identify

Our Family Values

—————————————

—————————————

—————————————

—————————————

—————————————

—————————————

—————————————

—————————————

—————————————

—————————————

—————————————

—————————————

—————————————

—————————————

three main values that guide their lives and why they chose those three. As they share their values, I write them down on a board, and by the time we're done, we usually have a pretty impressive list of values. Some all-time favorites are love, family, honesty, integrity, fairness, kindness, forgiveness, solidarity. The list goes on and on. The task of teaching your values to your children gives you a great opportunity to articulate clearly the values that guide your life. Therefore, before moving on to the next section, I encourage you to take a few moments to think about your own values. What are the ones that are most important to you and your family? Why? You can use the space on page 29 to record your thoughts. You will need these for your strategy building exercises in Chapter Five.

Values in Movies

Media messages have embedded values and points of view. This statement is one of the core principles that apply to all media, even the book you are holding in your hand. The point of view, or ideology of this book is colored by my Catholicism. This, of course, is on purpose. One value underlying this book is the importance of communication in the parent-child relationship. There are others as well. With a book such as this one, the point of view and underlying values should be fairly easy to spot. In other books, such as a novel, they might not be so obvious.

The same is true of every movie you and your children watch. In some films, such as the classic *Song of Bernadette,* point of view and values are easy to spot. More recently, *Bella* had a very straightforward pro-adoption message. These kinds of films or "message movies," while good and usually giving a message consistent with Christian morality and teaching, do not leave much room for the moral imagination. Some film reviewers consider these films too "preachy" to appeal to a large audience. That's okay with me because these kinds of films are fairly easy to speak about with your kids. The values are front and center.

More often, however, the values in a movie story are not so "in your face." Rather, they are hidden within the details of the story, between the lines, if you will, disguised or vague. With these films, it takes a bit more effort to discern and articulate the values present. Talking about these films is more challenging for a parent than the "message" films. Using your moral imagination, all those things you've learned and stored up from your multitude of experiences will aid you in making meaning from a film and help you identify the values present in it.

Making meaning from movies is covered in detail in Chapter Four. Here I will briefly say that not all the values you identify in a movie will be ones that you, as a Christian or Catholic parent, will want your kids to integrate into their lives. This does not automatically translate to mean that you should, therefore, exclude a particular movie from your child's experience. Being able to identify negative values in film and talking about them with your kids is just as important for their character development as identifying and talking about the positive values. For example, Disney's *The Lion King* was criticized as being racist because two of the three evil hyenas were voiced by minority actors (Whoopi Goldberg and Cheech Marin). Whether or not you agree with this criticism, racism, a negative value, is a topic worthy of conversation between parents and children.

I think it's important to say at this juncture that some parents may shy away from talking about movies with the kids because they think it will take the fun out of movie watching. And if you, as the parent, are a fun-spoiler, that doesn't bode well for a developing relationship. Make sure you allow the kids to have fun when they see a movie, whether at home or at the theater. Talking doesn't have to sap the fun. The aim is to have fun and learn at the same time.

Difficult Issues in Movies

Have you ever watched your child discover something for the first time? Her delight at the touch of grass on bare feet? His joy at splashing through puddles? Fascination and wonder are precious parts of childhood. Kids constantly ask questions. What's that? Why is it that way? One of the reasons you exercise the patience it takes to answer their persistent questions is because with each exchange you are building a relationship with them based on communication and trust.

Eventually, your children will ask difficult questions, and you will be challenged to answer them in a way they can understand, according to your values. Sometimes, these kinds of questions might be raised because they are present in a movie story. When movies depict such things as death, abuse, bullying, or certain aspects of relationships, you have an opportunity to speak with your child about these issues, in an age-appropriate manner, of course. Movies can provide a safe place for kids to ask questions about difficult issues. By relating to something happening in a movie story, rather than to themselves, they have the opportunity to explore an issue without it hitting too close to home.

A movie I use clips from all the time in my workshops is *Bridge to Terabithia*. I offer some questions for conversation based on this film in Chapter Seven. One of the difficult issues this film depicts is death. It also depicts how the characters in the story deal with it. This movie provides an opening to talk about death without your child having that concrete experience. It could help you explain death to her when she faces it in reality for the first time. Death is never easy to talk about, and with children it is even harder.

Another difficult issue presented in many movies is the treatment of the human body and sexuality. Related issues such as relationships, body image, sexual activity, dating, marriage, and family life are also prominent. A basic understanding of Pope John Paul II's teaching, *Theology of the Body*, can help you greatly in talking about these issues, especially with teenagers. In these matters, society's values are sometimes very different from Catholic values. Therefore, be clear with your kids about what the Church teaches and why it is important.

Movies can also bring up issues such as modesty, bullying, dealing with puberty, or a first crush. These and other issues are important to any parent trying to instill positive values in their children. The children will understand these issues in one way from how the movies depict them. Talking with them about how you see these issues will give them the chance to ask questions and understand them from the perspective of your values, not the movie's values.

SAINTS TO GUIDE US
Saint Edith Stein

Edith Stein's parents taught her values just as you are doing with your children. As a philosopher, she devoted much study to understanding the experience of values. When she became a Catholic, then a Carmelite, she strived to live by those values.

Edith Stein was born into a Jewish family, the youngest of eleven children, on October 12, 1891, in Breslau, Germany. As a teenager, she lost her faith in God and decided to give up praying. She excelled in school, a very intelligent girl. When she was accepted into Gottingen University, she studied philosophy under the tutelage of Edmund Husserl, founder of the philosophical school of phenomenology. Stein and those who follow phenomenology study experience itself, objectively and scientifically (Pope John Paul II was also of this philosophical school). Her doctoral thesis was entitled "The Problem of Empathy." In this work, after establishing that the person is individually both body and soul, she came to the conclusion that empathizing with another can expand our own values and understanding of ourselves.

While studying with Husserl, she met people who introduced her to Roman Catholicism, but she was still skeptical. A chance encounter left a deep impression on her. While with a friend visiting Frankfurt, they entered the cathedral there. Edith noticed a woman enter from the market. "This was something totally new to me. In the synagogues and Protestant churches I had visited people simply went to the services. Here, however, I saw someone coming straight from the busy marketplace into this empty church, as if she was going to have an intimate conversation. It was something I never forgot."[3]

On January 1, 1922, Edith's long road to Catholicism reached its goal in her Baptism. After this event, she went home and told her mother she was Catholic. Edith's conversion was a source of pain for her mother for the rest of her life. She wanted to enter the Carmelite convent immediately, but her spiritual mentor advised against it. She was only to get her wish in 1933. During the intervening decade, Edith taught at a Dominican sisters' school and was a frequent public

3. From *Life in a Jewish Family* translated by Josephine Koeppel, O.C.D., copyright © 1986 by Washington Province of Discalced Carmelites. ICS Publications, 2131 Lincoln Road, N.E., Washington, DC 20002-1199 U.S.A., www.icspublications.org.

speaker on women's issues. She also spent time translating some of the philosophical works of Saint Thomas Aquinas. During this time, she also continued to write, combining scholarship with faith.

She finally entered the Carmelites in Cologne on October 14, 1933. She took the name Sr. Teresa Benedicta of the Cross. She saw her vocation as being a call from God to intercede on behalf of everyone. As the German threat to the Jewish people increased, Edith increased her prayers for her people. When the Jewish people were subjected to the terror of the Nazis, Edith was smuggled across the German border to the Netherlands, to the Carmelite convent in Echt.

On August 2, 1942, the Gestapo came to the convent in Echt and arrested Edith and her sister, Rosa, who had also become Catholic. They were taken to the concentration camp at Auschwitz. It is believed that Edith was killed on August 9, 1942, in the gas chambers. This date is also her feast day.

Edith Stein was canonized a saint on October 11, 1998, by Pope John Paul II. Saint Edith Stein, pray for us.

QUESTIONS FOR FAMILY CONVERSATION

1. Pick a favorite story about Jesus from the Gospel and read it together as a family. What values did you notice Jesus practicing? How do you practice those same values in your life?

2. What is empathy? Can you think of examples from your own life when you have felt empathy toward another person? Share this story with your kids explaining empathy to them. Have they had experiences of empathy? Have them share those stories with you.

3. Next time you watch a movie, talk about the values of the movie. Do they agree with your values? Why or why not? How do you approach the negative values in a film?

4. Have each member of the family articulate three values they try to live by. Review together the list you made in the sidebar entitled Our Family Values on page 29. Talk about why they are important. Give examples of what the values look like when they are lived.

Chapter Three

How Movies Work

Storytelling

God created humans as social beings. Being and interacting with other people is part of what makes us human. Ever since the beginning of humanity, people have been communicating with one another through stories. Hieroglyphs and cave paintings depict the history of those who left them for future generations. Long before the advent of written languages, people communicated through storytelling. Even most parts of the Bible existed first as oral tradition, passed down through generations, centuries before being written down.

Stories form the fabric of life. By telling someone a story about yourself, you give that person a glimpse of who you are, the values you hold, and what is most important to you. Imagine introducing yourself to a stranger. What might be the first thing you tell that person? This communicates your priorities. If family is the most important thing to you, chances are you will describe yourself as a parent, maybe say how many kids you have. If work is foremost in your life, you might tell the person what you do and why you love it.

Besides being conduits of information, such as the values and priorities of the storyteller, stories can touch us deeply. They speak to our emotions and help us capture what it means to be human and in relationship with other people. Stories can move us to action. Did anyone tell you a story of injustice and you found yourself indignant and wanted to do something to right the wrong? Stories also help us empathize with other people, to be able to see something from another's perspective. Even more powerfully and pertinent to this time and culture, stories can provide a safe place in which to speak of difficult issues.

Our faith is based in story. Starting with Genesis right through Revelation, story after story tells about God's interaction with people. God breaks into human history in so many wonderful ways that, if you're anything like me, you never get tired of hearing the stories. The greatest story, of course, is Jesus himself, the Word of God made flesh. After Jesus ascended to the Father, the Church continued telling the story to whomever would listen and still tells it even today. The story itself has not changed, but people have developed myriad ways to tell it.

Whether the story be sacred or secular (or both), one popular storytelling method today is film.

Movies: The Art of Visual Storytelling

Filmmaking is an art form. You may not consider the latest Hollywood blockbuster to be a work of art, but each film in its own way contains the elements of an artist's creation. What is unique about film is that it is always a team effort as witnessed by the length of the credits at the end of a film. The director is the primary artist, the one who wields the brush and has the last word, but without the supporting team of people, no film would be possible.

As you read on, please remember this: not every film I use as an example to illustrate a point is appropriate viewing for children. If you are not familiar with a particular film, use your family media strategy (to be developed in Chapter Five) to help you choose whether or not to view it.

The Filmmaker's Canvas: The Story

Just as there would be no painting without a subject to paint, there would be no film without a story, otherwise known as the plot. Here are some elements to look for in a good story.

1. Unified Story Line

For a film story to make sense, the viewer needs to understand what is going on. The best films are focused on only one story, a single thread that runs throughout the film with a beginning, middle, and end. If there is too much happening, too many characters doing unrelated things, the audience gets confused. Confused audiences usually mean bad news at the box office.

To better understand the concept of a unified story line, check out the deleted scenes from your favorite films. These can usually be found with the special features on the DVD/Blu-Ray disc of the film. When viewing them after seeing the movie, you can usually tell why they were left out. The scene might be great, but it seems extra. If there is a director's commentary available for the deleted scenes, he/she will sometimes remark that the scene was fine, but it did nothing to help the story along.

2. The Story Is Believable

In order for a movie to catch its audience's attention, it has to connect to their experience. The movie *Nim's Island*, although it has elements that are unrealistic, is ultimately about a child missing a parent. Family life is something that the majority of people have experienced at one time or another in their lives and can relate to. The story is believable because it makes sense as a possible real-life experience.

But there are some movies that do not conform to the way things are. Rather, they may give us a glimpse of the way in which things could be better. An example of this kind of film might be *The Blind Side*, starring Sandra Bullock. This movie tells the story of the Tuohy family and the homeless young man they invite into their family. The goodness of the Tuohys gives the audience a glimpse of the way things could be.

What about all the films that are totally unbelievable such as *Star Wars* or *Avatar*? Even these have something recognizable or else audiences would dismiss them. These kinds of films tend to create a world of their own where the strange things that happen seem believable in their created environment. The *Harry Potter* and *Twilight Saga* film series (and the books before them) created a specific kind of world for their characters to inhabit. Even so, there are familiar elements to each plot such as the experience of going to school, entering into relationships, and the journey of discovering who one is as a person. These are the elements that make these kinds of stories believable even though our real world never was and never will be like it.

3. The Story Has to Be Interesting

Interest is very subjective. One person may be bored stiff by what interests someone else. Here are some tricks that filmmakers use to attract and keep your attention.

Suspense. I don't only mean the kind of suspense you find in thrillers or horror films. That is obvious suspense, but also the kind that just has the viewer wondering what is going to happen next or how the character will solve a dilemma. *E.T.: The Extra-Terrestrial* has plenty of suspense. When one thing happens and you think it's the end, there is another twist to keep you on the edge of your seat.

Action. Just like suspense, some action is obvious: car chases, explosions, good guys pursued by bad guys (or the other way around!), or the boat sinking. But there is more to action than eye-pleasing special and visual effects used in movie making. Action can also be internal, within the minds and emotions of the characters. I saw a film by aboriginal Australian filmmaker Warwick Thornton, called *Samson & Delilah.* It explored the developing relationship of two aboriginal teenagers. There were few words in the movie, yet the action was captured on the faces of the actors and the intensity of emotion they conveyed. Granted, internal action films will probably not be very interesting for children. You can keep them for yourself to enjoy when the kids are otherwise occupied.

Humor. Yes, one of the purposes of movies, albeit not the most profound, is to bring us out of ourselves, enabling viewers to get away from real life for a couple of hours and just be entertained. Humor is one of those things that makes movie-going so much fun. I like tongue-in-cheek humor, such as is found in the *Indiana Jones* films. I'm also a sometimes fan of Robin Williams. He was really funny in *Robots* (as the voice of Fender) as well as in *RV,* an over-the-top story made believable by Williams' comedic expertise. When I first saw the classic *The Princess Bride*, my reaction was "It's so stupid, it's funny," but it grew on me. Watching it with a group of friends helps, too! Now it's one of those funny movies that I like to watch when I'm having a bad day or just feeling stressed out (along with *Galaxy Quest*). Kids love humor, too, although sometimes their style of humor is not the same as what most adults appreciate.

The Filmmaker's Subject: The Characters

We could write a whole book about characterization in film, but I'll just mention a few tidbits. Without interesting characters to inhabit the story, there would be no film. There are many ways to establish characters. One of the easiest is through appearance. For example, Captain Jack Sparrow (Johnny Depp) in the *Pirates of the Caribbean* films is an unstable, eccentric character, and you could probably guess this just by his appearance. Change the costume and you get a different feel for the character. Characters can also be defined by their actions. Is the character good or bad? How can you tell? Modern filmmaking often blurs the lines of good and bad, right and wrong. In *Spider Man 3*, Sandman (Thomas Haden Church) does bad things, but he really is not a bad person and has many good qualities. This changes how we feel about him as a "bad guy."

Another method of characterization is to compare a character with his or her antagonist. In the *Harry Potter* films, you have the innocence of Harry Potter (Daniel Radcliffe) against the evil of Lord

Voldemort (Ralph Fiennes). In *Star Trek*, we find the contrast between Spock (Zachary Quinto) and Nero (Eric Bana) as well as the conflict between Spock and Kirk (Chris Pine). The ways the characters resolve conflicts gives the audience insight into the characters.

These ways of defining character are all fascinating, but the most important thing is how a character develops throughout the film. Did the character grow during the course of the movie or not? The Oscar-winning film *Slumdog Millionaire* focused on two brothers. One was a developing character who tried to make the best of his life in the midst of the most difficult circumstances. The other brother was a static character who let himself be taken over by the same circumstances. Character development is a great perspective from which to talk about a film. What were the character's choices? How did those choices influence what happened? Would you make different choices given the same circumstances?

If you are interested in learning more about what goes into the making of a film, there is an excellent full-length documentary on the special features disc of the DVD release of *Star Wars Episode III: Revenge of the Sith*. It's entitled *Within a Minute* and it's the most in-depth presentation I've seen on everything and everyone involved in the making of less than one minute of film. You don't have to be a *Star Wars* fan to appreciate the intricacies of the filmmaking process. There are also many books available on the making of films, including many Disney classics and films such as *The Chronicles of Narnia*. Just browse through the film section of your local bookstore.

The Filmmaker's Brushes: Film Techniques

The techniques used in making a film are fascinating and many. When I first began studying film, I thought that understanding the techniques employed would lessen my enjoyment of going to the movies. On the contrary, understanding how films are put together has made the experience of watching a film even greater for me.

1. Visual Design

Color vs. Black and White. Before the dawn of color TV and movies, black and white was the default. So now that we have color, why use black and white? Watch *Schindler's List.* Black and white becomes a symbol of the bleakness of the subject matter. What little color there is in the film is used to great effect. *The Wizard of Oz* moves from black and white to color and then back again as a technique to let you know where you are. Black and white is Kansas and color is Oz.

Set Design and Costumes. Many filmmakers prefer to work on location as often as they can for the realism effect, but often studio sets must substitute for the real thing. In set design, nothing is by accident. For example, in the *Lord of the Rings* films, Bag End was decorated in such a way so that the audience knew what Bilbo (Ian Holm) was like just by seeing the environment. Likewise the costumes for Frodo (Elijah Wood) were of burgundy and gold tones, as he was the leader, and Sam's (Sean Astin) costume was made of more earthy tones, as he was the servant and worked the earth.

Lighting. Most prominent among visual techniques is lighting. The way the actors or set is lit can determine what kind of emotional effect the scene will have on the audience. Are the actors cast in shadow? Is it night or day, indoors or outdoors? Is the light soft, emitting a warm feeling or is it harsh lighting such as one might find in a hospital scene, leaving the viewer feeling disconcerted or disoriented? Does the light come from above or below, the side or straight on? The answer to each question goes far to determine the dramatic effect of the shot.

2. Cinematography

Framing. Cinematography is anything that has to do with the camera. Framing a shot is deciding what is going to be in the picture and what's not. It also decides what or who is in the foreground or the background. The way a shot is framed can determine what catches our attention on screen. Often times the eye sees only what is in the foreground and the background action goes by unnoticed or vice versa. To get an idea of framing, see the Frame It activity in Chapter Six.

Camera Angles. Camera angles (sometimes called camera shots) are key to making a shot deliver what the director intends. There are wide angles to establish a scene as a panoramic view, close-ups that convey intimacy, shots from above which make the subject look smaller, or shots from below which make the subject look bigger or taller, such as was often used for Hagrid (Robbie Coltrane) in the *Harry Potter* films. The placement of the camera can also determine point of view. Many times the camera acts as narrator, but sometimes the camera becomes the eyes of one of the characters and only sees what she sees.

Camera Movement. Camera movement when holding the camera is called panning. You can pan left or right, up or down to sweep across a shot. Zooming in draws the subject closer, while zooming out moves the subject further away. When the camera is mounted on a track, the movement is called tracking and results in a smooth movement. Recently, I learned another technique of camera movement. I watched some of the extras on the *Star Trek* DVD and found one that showed how the director got the shaking movement for the space travel. While the camera person was aiming the camera, the director would lightly drum with his hands on the camera to give the shot the desired amount of shakiness!

3. Effects and Editing

Special Effects. Special effects actually happen on the set. If nature doesn't provide fog for a scene, it can be piped in. Making rain, wind, waves in a tank, or explosions are also special effects. A ship named *Charlotte* was built and then blown up for the film *National Treasure.* They had only one opportunity to do it, so they had seven cameras enclosed in Plexiglas at various points around the set to capture the action from different angles. The explosives experts had rigged everything up making sure all safety precautions had been implemented. When all was ready, the director yelled "action," and the ship went up in smoke!

Visual Effects. Visual effects, on the other hand, are any effects that are done by computer. CGI, or computer generated images, are widely used in movies. Visual effects could be anything from enhancing a natural location with more trees or a building, to filling up a sports stadium with spectators, to the creation of completely new characters. Technology has advanced so fast that visual effects people are continually coming up with new ways to make the impossible happen on screen. In the *Lord of the Rings* trilogy of films, the character Gollum (Andy Serkis) is totally computer generated. Through motion capture technology, an actor's performance is captured on the computer and transformed into the character. James Cameron used this technique to great effect in *Avatar.* These effects have gotten so good that sometimes the viewer can't tell the difference between the real image and the computer generated one.

Editing. This is where the movie really comes together. After the filming is done, it gets "cut" into the movie's final form. In most scenes, more than one take has been shot. The editor, in cooperation with the director, takes all the parts of the film and decides which ones end up in the final cut. This can be a painstaking process as most filmmakers shoot hundreds of hours of film only to cut it all down to a two-hour film. The superfluous material is put aside. Action films require an editor to make very fast cuts, making images appear in rapid succession whereas more dramatic films generally feature slower cuts.

4. Sound and Music

Sound Effects. The more movies I watch, the more I am fascinated by sound. Very few of the sounds heard in a film are captured during the actual filming. Some might be, for example the dialogue, although the actors regularly have to return during post-production to re-record at least part of their dialogue if it did not record clearly during filming. This process is called ADR, automatic dialogue replacement. But most other sounds are recorded in post-production, after filming is finished. Every sound from a telephone ringing or a TV in the background, to the clashes of swords or footsteps, is added to the film by the sound editor. Sound effects are essential to every film. Try this the next time you watch an action sequence in a film. First watch it as-is and note your reaction. Watch the scene a second time with the volume turned down all the way. Note how different your emotional reaction is to the scene without sound.

Music. A key component to every film, Music appeals directly to our emotions. We hear sounds through the little bones in our ears, and the effect goes directly into the part of the brain that processes emotion. Music plays a big part in how film is able to manipulate emotions. Often during a romantic scene, you will hear soft, flowing music, heavy on strings. The camera will be close to the subjects. Together these elicit an emotional response from the viewer. Action sequences are commonly accompanied by louder music, with an emphasis on brass instruments to convey a sense of urgency or suspense. A good example of the use of music in film is in *Cast Away*. While Chuck (Tom Hanks) is on the island, there is no music. This technique gives the impression that you are sharing his isolation. Only when he leaves the island does the music swell, and, along with the character, the viewer feels the sadness of leaving the security of the island.

SAINTS TO GUIDE US
Saint Juan Diego

The techniques of visual filmmaking are always developing. The use of images, however, goes far back into history. In our own Catholic heritage, images have always played an important role in devotion. One of the most revered is the miraculous image of Our Lady of Guadalupe on the tilma (or cloak) of Juan Diego.

In 1474, at the height of the Aztec Empire, Cuauhtlatoatzin (Koo-ah-ooh-tla-toe-at-zeen), now known as Saint Juan Diego, was born in what is now Mexico. It was a time of political upheaval when the Spanish conquistadors overthrew the Emperor Montezuma II. But other Spaniards, the Franciscan Friars, had come to the New World looking not for earthly power, but to bring the Gospel of Jesus Christ to the native peoples of Mexico.

Among the tribes visited by the Friars were the Nahua to which Juan Diego belonged. They lived about fifteen miles north of Mexico City. Juan Diego was lowly and ordinary, a farmer and weaver. Having heard the message of salvation from the priest Father Peter de Gand, Cuauhtlatoatzin was baptized and given the name of Juan Diego. He was fifty years old.

In order to continue learning about his new-found faith, Juan Diego walked fifteen miles into Mexico City to receive instruction and attend Mass. On December 9, 1531, during one of these walks that took him past Tepeyac Hill, he heard music. Upon investigating, he was greeted by a young Aztec princess, who said she was the Virgin

Mary. She asked Juan Diego to go to the bishop and ask that a church be built in her honor on the hill. He did as requested, but with no social standing he had to wait hours to see the bishop. When he was finally received and had told the whole story, the bishop was skeptical. Juan Diego returned again the next day with the same results. This time the bishop asked that Juan Diego bring proof of what he was saying.

The following day Juan Diego missed his appointment with the Lady, going instead for a priest for his sick uncle. She met him along the path, reassured him that his uncle was cured, and told him to climb to the top of the hill where he would find the proof the bishop needed. In his cloak he gathered the flowers blooming there and set off for the bishop's house once again. Upon opening his cloak, Castilian roses, which did not grow in Mexico, cascaded to

the floor. The bishop, however, only had eyes for the image that had appeared on Juan Diego's cloak, the image of Our Lady of Guadalupe.

Shortly afterwards, the church was built on Tepeyac Hill in honor of Our Lady of Guadalupe. Juan Diego was given permission to live in a small house next to the church, to be its caretaker and to welcome pilgrims. He lived there in humility and holiness until his death in 1548 at the age of seventy-four. He was canonized a saint by Pope John Paul II on July 31, 2002.

Juan Diego's cloak hangs in the Basilica of Our Lady of Guadalupe in Mexico City to this day. Over the years, the image and its story have been an effective form of evangelization. In Juan Diego's day, while preaching did not yield understanding among the native Mexican population, this image was enthusiastically embraced and evoked a deep devotion that is still evident in Mexican culture. Saint Juan Diego, pray for us.

QUESTIONS FOR FAMILY CONVERSATION

1. What are some favorite stories in your family? What elements of the story make them so memorable? How might you make your story into a movie?

2. Choose one of the kids' favorite films. Talk together about the main characters. How do you know about the character? His appearance? What he does? Does the character grow during the film or stay the same? Why do you like or not like the character?

3. After learning about film techniques, which one is most fascinating for you? If you were going to work on a movie, which

job would you like? Would it be working the camera, editing, doing effects, or recording the sound? Look for that film technique in the next movie you watch.

4. Making movies is a team effort. When you do things together as a family, do you work as a team? Is it easy to be part of a team or do you sometimes find it hard? What happens when someone on the team does not contribute as agreed?

Chapter Four

Making Meaning from Movies

Content and Context

When it comes to making meaning out of a movie, the difference between content and context is crucial. Content is what makes up the movie, its story line, words, and images. This is what the Motion Picture Association of America (MPAA) ratings are based on. Ratings will be covered in more detail later in the chapter. Context is what happens within the story of the movie, the subtext, its setting (time and place), the societal rules in place, the interplay between characters, the motivations behind a character's actions, the development (or not) of the characters, and so much more. To get at the deeper meaning of a film, you have to look not only at the content but the context as well.

Among the people with whom I have had the pleasure of doing film dialogue, content is sometimes a contentious point. For many people, the "big three" when it comes to judging whether a movie is good or not, or if it is appropriate for children, are instances of sex, offensive language, and violence in the content of the film. Because morality and passing on of values is such an important part of Catholic and Christian living, these things are of concern to thoughtful movie-goers. Even so, they should not be the only criteria used when judging a movie. Solely using incidents of sex, language, or violence (or lack thereof) in making decisions about movies is to see only the content of the film. To say that a movie is good just because it *does not* have offensive language, sex, or violence, such as a G-rated film, does not take into account what the movie *does* have, its context. For example, *Finding Nemo*, a touching story of a father's search for his missing son (even if they are fish), is rated G. However, the negative depiction of the female characters is problematic. The mama fish is dead, Dory (voice of Ellen DeGeneres) is a ditz, and Darla (voice of Lulu Ebeling), the dentist's niece, is absolutely horrible. Thoughtful movie-goers take into account both the content and the context of the film.

To get at the context of a film, one endeavors to read between the lines, look for character development, notice the symbolism contained in the film's motifs, and so much more. If you decide to stop at content, you may miss a multitude of opportunities to allow a movie to speak to you or your children in meaningful ways through reflection on the context.

For example, the 2007 movie *Transformers* is a reflection about the struggle for freedom and the abuse or proper use of power, among other things. By portraying an extreme situation, "good guy" alien robots coming to Earth to protect humans from "bad guy" alien robots, the movie shows front and center the consequences of abuse of power. The movie gives people an opportunity to look into themselves and consider their own need for forgiveness for even small abuses of whatever power they may have. The movie also has something to say about true strength and protection of those who are weak. All these elements make it a wonderful movie to talk about in a group setting such as a parish youth group or preparation for Confirmation class. I have used the movie both with young people and adults and had meaningful conversations. With the adults we talked about what it means to have power and how it can be very easy to use that power for our own ends. With the kids, we talked about what true strength is and how Jesus asks those who are strong to protect and care for those who are not. These conversations arose from trying to get at the context of the movie. While acknowledging the elements that gave the movie a PG-13 rating, intense violence and some offensive language, we would have missed the opportunity to draw significant meaning from the movie if we had stopped at the movie's content.

A Note About Ratings

Ratings are useful tools when deciding whether or not a film is appropriate for your children. They offer information to help guide your choices. Most films released in the United States are given a rating by the Motion Picture Association of America. In Canada, each province has its own ratings board. Please see Chapter Seven for the Web sites of these groups. Each Web site lists the criteria used in establishing ratings. Knowing the criteria helps when you consider a film's rating.

While ratings can be helpful, they are only a tool, one of many in your parental toolbox, for deciding whether or not a particular film is appropriate for your child. The rating will only indicate content, whether or not and to what degree there is offensive language, sex, or violence present in the film. The rating does not speak to the value of the meaning that can be gleaned from reflection on the context of the film. Other tools for your toolbox will be covered in Chapter Five.

Form and Genre in Film

Literary Forms

When it comes to making meaning from movies, hearkening back to your high school literature class can help. Because movies are stories, the principles used in literary analysis can also apply to film (with some extra consideration for the visual aspects). Recognizing a literary form in a movie goes a long way on the journey of discovering its meaning.

Analogy. Definition: inference that if two or more things agree with one another in some respects there will probably be agreement in others. Usually you will find "like" or "as" in a sentence containing an analogy. For example, the heart is like a bicycle pump. One forces blood into our veins and the other forces air into bike tires. Recognizing the use of analogy in film already gives an indication of its meaning.

One analogy that is commonly used in film is the journey motif. Life is like a journey. When a character in a film takes a journey from one place to the other, they are often taking a journey in their life as well. A good example of this is *Clueless.* For the first time in her comfortable, superficial life, Cher (Alicia Silverstone) is challenged to discover her deeper self. When overwhelmed by the task, she journeys to and through the mall, her place of refuge and comfort. Movement from one place to the other gives her time to contemplate her life. During the journey, she finally realizes what she's been missing.

So, when you run across a movie with some kind of journey (it doesn't have to be a physical journey, it could be mental or spiritual), it's a fair bet that some of the meaning will come from the journey analogy.

Metaphor. Definition: a figure of speech in which a word or phrase literally denoting one kind of object or idea is used in place of another to suggest a likeness or analogy between them (as in *drowning in money*). Metaphor comes so naturally to us that we often don't notice we are using it. I used one earlier in this chapter: food for thought. I remember telling my brother when I knew he was getting in trouble that he was "headed for the dog house."

Metaphor in film is a little more difficult to get at. Since metaphor asks us to think figuratively instead of literally, there's much more room for interpretation when it comes to pinning down (another metaphor) the meaning of a movie. A movie story can mean something different to each person who experiences it, depending on their outlook on life, situation, and background. So we ask it questions: What is the meaning of this movie metaphor? Going back to the definition: What is the similar thing being replaced by the metaphor the movie is presenting?

Life as a House is a movie about a metaphor. George Monroe (Kevin Kline) is dying of cancer and he wants to connect with his estranged son, Sam (Hayden Christensen). George's plan is to tear down his shack of a house and rebuild it with Sam's help. The process of tearing down and rebuilding becomes a metaphor for his life and his relationship with Sam.

Parable. Definition: a usually short fictitious story that illustrates a moral attitude or a religious principle. Catholics are familiar with the concept of parable from those found in the Gospels and preached about at Sunday Mass, the most famous and beloved being the parable of the Prodigal Son. We listen to the story and reflect on what it means in our lives.

When movie stories can be thought of as parables, there is usually an obvious message, a moral to the story. Movie parables can also be thought of as message movies. The classic fantasy movie, *Edward Scissorhands*, tells a story about welcoming those different from us and treating them with respect. *Wall-E*, about a cute, garbage collecting robot, has a definite environmental message, reflecting the themes of Catholic social teaching. Both films could

With older children, a great way to look at a film is through the lens of Catholic social teaching. The Church has had a consistent teaching beginning with Pope Leo XIII's *Rerum Novarum* in 1891 through today. Here are the themes and one question for each (out of many) you might pose to a film. For a detailed explanation of the themes, you can go to the Web site of the United States Conference of Catholic Bishops: www.usccb. org/sdwp/projects/socialteaching/ excerpt.shtml.

• Life and Dignity of the Human Person: Is the dignity of the human person reflected in the film?

• Call to Family, Community, and Participation: Do people help one another in the film?

• Rights and Responsibilities: Do the characters show responsibility toward one another and society?

• Option for the Poor and Vulnerable: Are the needs of the weak met?

• The Dignity of Work and the Rights of Workers: How is work portrayed: as a way to participate in society or only to make a living?

• Solidarity: Are justice and peace sought in the film? Do the characters love their neighbor?

• Care for God's Creation: Are the resources of the earth respected or abused in the film?

be thought of as parables. Even *Pirates of the Caribbean: Curse of the Black Pearl* can be seen as a parable about greed, couched in a funny action-adventure movie.

Genre

Just as literature has its different categories of stories or genres, such as romance, science fiction, or mystery, based on the narrative elements of the story, so does film. Being able to identify a film's genre is a big step in the meaning-making process. Movie genres are not as black and white as they used to be. Innovations in narrative and film techniques have blurred the boundaries of traditional genres. Here I will only cover the most basic genres.

Documentary. Probably the most basic distinction in genre is between documentaries and fiction. The subjects of documentaries are usually real people, historical events, or issues. Documentaries chronicle an event or a person's life or look at different sides of an issue. Their main purpose is to inform the audience of some real-life person, happening, or topic of interest. Some recent documentaries that have received a lot of attention are Michael Moore's political commentary films, *Capitalism* and *Fahrenheit 9/11*. Not as many documentaries are made for wide theatrical distribution as are fiction films. Many documentaries can be found on specialty television channels such as The History Channel, The Biography Channel, and Discovery Channel. Making meaning of documentaries is not that difficult, but good questions to ask when viewing a documentary are: What is the worldview presented in this film? Is it the only one? Have any voices been left out of the treatment of the subject?

Action/Adventure. These kinds of films are usually big-budget, rather physical movies, with fights, car chases, explosions, and nonstop action. They usually have a simple good guy (girl) vs. bad guy (girl) story line where the good guy constantly has to overcome the obstacles put in his way by the bad guy. For the most part, action/adventure films are pure entertainment and audience pleasers and are not meant to have a lot of deeper meaning, although some of them do. Some good examples of films in this genre are the *Indiana Jones* films, *Adventures of Robin Hood* (Errol Flynn), and *Zorro* movies.

Comedy. Comedies aim to make us laugh. They range from slapstick and spoofs to satire and dark comedy. One of the most popular subgenres of comedy is the romantic comedy, a funny story based on a relationship of some kind. As in the case of action/adventure films, comedies are usually not out to make a deep statement, but to entertain. This, however, does not mean that you cannot glean meaning from comedies. Examples of some family comedies are *Cheaper by the Dozen* and *Evan Almighty*.

Drama. These serious, plot-driven movies make up the largest genre of films. Most of the time dramatic stories are more realistic than their comedy or fantasy counterparts. Dramas focus on development of character within the story. Oftentimes, dramas are rich in symbolism. Understanding the symbolism in a film is part of the meaning-making process in drama. There are many subgenres of drama including biopics (movies about someone's life), crime dramas, epics, war movies, historical films, and westerns. *Remember the Titans*, a teen film, is a good example of a sports drama. Interestingly enough, most children's movies fall into some other category.

Thriller/Horror. These are the scary ones. Thrillers and horror films dredge up our fears in terrifying, shocking ways but manage to entertain at the same time. Thrillers tend to be scary in a more anticipatory way, whereas horror tends to show all the blood and gore. Some of the old silent films of Dracula fit into this genre. Today, movie monsters tend to be more sophisticated and the films use many computer generated effects. *Jaws, Rear Window*, and *Psycho* are classic thrillers. Horror and thriller films are usually too scary for younger children. True, there might be some scary elements in children's films such as any of the *Harry Potter* movies or *The Wizard of Oz* (flying monkeys freaked me out as a kid!), but overall they belong to the fantasy genre.

Musicals. When characters in a movie break out in song or begin to dance around the scene, it's pretty obvious you are in a musical. Many times, musicals display more light-heartedness than a drama, although this is not always the case. For example, the musical *Moulin Rouge!* fits better into the dark drama genre. I grew up watching *Oklahoma* and *The Sound of Music.* There was the era of the teen musicals with *Grease, Footloose*, and *Fame.* Most Disney animated films such as *Aladdin* and *The Lion King* fall into the musical genre. The past decade has seen the comeback of the musical with *High School Musical, Hairspray*, and *Mamma Mia.* All musicals also fit into whatever genre the movie would be if it didn't have singing and dancing. Thus *The Sound of Music* is also a drama, even more specifically, a biopic about Maria Von Trapp.

Science Fiction/Fantasy. This genre displays the most imagination of all the film genres. Sci-fi films are usually futuristic, based in science but going way beyond. Their fantastical, made-up worlds are peopled with heroes, villains, aliens, and monsters. They include impossible missions, improbable scenarios, and the potential of technology. Science fiction and fantasy are often very closely entwined, such as the famous *Star Wars* and *Star Trek* series. Most films made from comic books also fit into sci-fi/fantasy. This genre often poses to the viewer very fundamental human and ethical questions in the guise of other-worldly stories. Some very popular films in this genre include *Avatar*, *Wall-E*, *The Twilight Saga*, and classics such as *The Day the Earth Stood Still*. Many children's movies fit into this genre, such as *Enchanted*, *Bridge to Terabithia*, and *E.T.: The Extra-Terrestrial*.

Asking Questions:
The Media Mindfulness Strategy

The most important tool when making meaning from a movie is one your children have been using since they could speak: the question. Many of the concerns Catholic parents have in regard to the media's influence on their children can be addressed by asking them questions and entering into meaningful conversations about the media they consume. When the children are younger, the questions need to be posed by the parents to encourage interaction with media. As the kids grow older, they will be able to formulate the questions for themselves.

For younger kids, simple questions are appropriate. Did you like the movie? Why? Who was your favorite character? Why? What did you like or not like about what they did? Very young children are not yet capable of analytical thinking, to discover on their own what a movie means. As a parent, you can ask age-appropriate questions to get them to think about their movie experiences. When they get a little older, around eight to ten years old, the questions of the media mindfulness circle presented on page 63 will help them enter into critical thinking.

Discovering meaning by asking questions of movies is somewhat of a novelty for most adults and kids. Of course, you don't ask the questions *during* the movie but enter into conversation afterward. Asking questions of the media seems strange to some people. My brother, the father of three, told me once that movies are just for fun and you take all the fun out of it for kids if you start asking them to think about what they saw. To some it might seem that this is indeed the case, but those who embrace finding the sacred in the secular can see the value of being active, critical thinkers when it comes to children and movies.

The media mindfulness strategy is a guide to asking questions for people of faith who desire to instill in their children the ability to engage in media, question it, and make media decisions based on

faith and values. These skills aid children as they discover life and interact with a society that does not always support and encourage Gospel values.

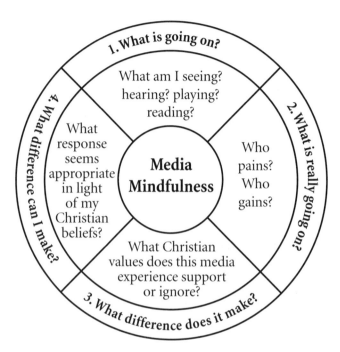

The media mindfulness strategy uses four questions: 1. What is going on? 2. What is really going on? 3. What difference does it make? 4. What difference can I make? Let's take a classic children's movie, *The Wizard of Oz*, and look at it from the perspective of these four questions.

1. What is going on? What am I seeing and hearing? With these questions, we look at the content of the story. In *The Wizard of Oz*, what's going on is that a tornado lands Dorothy in the magical Land of Oz. While trying to find a way home, she

---

1. Gretchen Hailer, *Believing in a Media Culture,* copyright © 1996 by Saint Mary's Press, www.smp.org. Used with permission.

meets the Scarecrow, the Cowardly Lion, and the Tin Man, who also need assistance. They go together to see the Wizard, who turns out to be a fake, so Glinda, the good witch, sends Dorothy home.

2. What is *really* going on? What underlies this story? Who suffers? Who gains? With these questions the viewer tries to understand the context of the story, not just the content. In this film, Dorothy is discovering who she is. She and her friends move from fear into confidence in themselves during their adventure, flying monkeys notwithstanding! Glinda tells Dorothy she has always had the power to go home and the ruby slippers become a symbol of Dorothy's trust in herself and her friends.

3. What difference does it make? What Christian values does this media experience support or ignore? In *The Wizard of Oz*, the value of family comes out very strongly: "There's no place like home." Courage is another, as is the contrast between good and evil. In many films today, the line between good and evil, right and wrong is often blurred and what's right or wrong is not as easily recognized. For example, one thing modern media does is normalize behavior. If you go strictly by the media, then it's normal to use profanity, or use whatever means necessary to get what you want. But is that what Jesus teaches us? No. Asking questions about the behavior and values depicted in a film can move you and your child into conversation about what you believe are proper Christian behavior and values.

4. What difference can *I* make? What response seems appropriate in light of my Christian beliefs? In my experience, this question can be the most difficult to answer. The answer to this question is where the movie meets real life. All the things you have discovered about the movie, its genre, character development, techniques, values, and meaning culminate in this

question. This question asks for a commitment from you in response to the movie you have just experienced. For children seeing *The Wizard of Oz*, a possible answer could be, "When I see someone being treated unfairly at school, I won't be afraid. I'll have courage to do what is right." Then you could discuss what action might be taken in this situation such as befriending that person or reporting the bad treatment to a teacher. Another answer to the question could be as simple as praying for people in the same situation as depicted in a film, such as praying for victims of natural disasters. When I saw the Oscar-winning film, *The Hurt Locker*, I resolved to pray for military personnel in EOD (explosive ordinance disposal) units and for a change in mentality so that they would not be needed in the future.

Using these four questions as a guide can turn your fun, movie-watching time with your children into an opportunity to grow in communication as a family, to pass on your values to your kids, and to help them use the answers to the questions to make positive media choices in the future. [The media mindfulness circle can be found on the Media Mindfulness tab at www.JClubCatholic.org.]

SAINTS TO GUIDE US
Blessed James Alberione

Looking at movies through the eyes of faith and values and discovering meaning in them is not a new concept. Evangelization with the media is the mission Blessed James Alberione gave to the religious communities he founded at the beginning of the twentieth century.

James Alberione was born in a little town in northern Italy called San Lorenzo di Fossano in 1884. Even as a little boy he knew he wanted to be a priest. While in the high school seminary at Bra, however, he did some reading that negatively influenced him and, unexpectedly, James found himself dismissed from the seminary program. Later, through the guidance and influence of his parish priest, he applied and was admitted to the seminary of the Diocese of Alba.

At age sixteen, on the night that separated the nineteenth and twentieth centuries, December 31, 1900, he prayed for four hours before the Blessed Sacrament at the Alba Cathedral. During that intense prayer, he was inspired to do something for the people of the century just beginning. Over the next decade, he finished his seminary studies, was ordained, did some parish work, and eventually became a teacher and spiritual director at the Alba Seminary.

During that time, the inspiration that began on the night between the centuries became clearer. He wanted to reach more than just his local people with the message of the Gospel. He wanted to make it known to all people through the most rapid forms of communication available. In 1914, he founded the Society of Saint Paul, and in 1915, the Daughters of Saint Paul. These consecrated men and women would use the media to promote the Gospel. Father Alberione chose Saint Paul as their patron because Paul was a great communicator of the Gospel and had used the media of his day, letter writing, to get the message out to as many people and countries as possible. In the end, Father Alberione founded ten institutes that became known as the Pauline Family.

Among the many media projects initiated by Father Alberione was San Paolo Films. Movies had only been around since 1895, so in 1938 when San Paolo Films began, it was still a very young industry. Father Alberione understood the influence of film and so wanted to pioneer films that would educate and inspire audiences. He was what would now be called the executive producer of the 1939 movie *Abuna Messias* about Cardinal William Massaia, the first missionary to Ethiopia. San Paolo Films made short catechetical films as well. In the early 1960s, three feature-length biblical films were produced: *The Great Leaders: Gideon and Samson*; *Jacob: The Man Who Fought with God*; and *Saul and David*. English language versions were distributed in the United States and are still available today. By 1985, after decades as Italy's major distributor of film entertainment to educational, professional, and church institutions, San Paolo Films was replaced by San Paolo Audiovisual to focus on material for home video release.

At the beginning of his media ministry, most Church leaders did not understand why Father Alberione would choose to focus on the media. However, as the Church's understanding of the importance of the media grew, so did respect for Father Alberione and his vision. Pope Paul VI, on June 28, 1969, two years before Father Alberione's death, visited the members of the Pauline Family. He had this to say about Father Alberione:

> There he is: humble, silent, tireless, always vigilant, recollected in his thoughts, which run from prayer to action; always intent on scrutinizing the "signs of the times," that is, the most creative ways to reach souls. Our Father Alberione has given the Church new instruments with which to express herself, new means to give vigor and breadth to her apostolate, new capacities and a new awareness of the validity and possibilities of her mission in the modern world with modern means. Dear Father Alberione, allow the Pope to rejoice in your long, faithful and tireless work and in the fruits it has produced for the glory of God and the good of the Church.

Father Alberione died at the age of eighty-seven on November 26, 1971. He was proclaimed blessed by Pope John Paul II on April 27, 2003. Blessed James Alberione, pray for us.

QUESTIONS FOR FAMILY CONVERSATION

The media mindfulness circle provides plenty of questions for family conversation.

1. Talk about the genre of some of your family's favorite movies. What elements of the movie clued you in to the genre? What did you expect or not expect just because of the genre?

For parents:

2. The media mindfulness circle will work well with your older children (eight and above). What kinds of questions might you ask the younger kids during a movie that would achieve age-appropriate responses to the circle's questions?
3. When questions bring to light the negative values present in a film, how will these be addressed?

Chapter Five

Developing a Family Strategy

Motivating Factors

Before we get into the details of the strategy, let's just take a moment to revisit and summarize why creating this strategy is a good thing. First, media are everywhere; media's influence is unavoidable. The question is: what are you going to do about that? It is how you respond to media that makes all the difference between a negative or positive experience of media (remember, the Church calls media gifts of God). You care enough about your parental responsibilities that you've picked up this book. You care enough to teach your child how to question the media, to identify its values, and to compare them with yours, otherwise you wouldn't have made it this far.

Second, the life skills provided by talking about media will be invaluable to your children's development all along the road. The communication between you and them during the formative years of their lives will set a pattern that will stay with them, enabling them to talk to you about the things that really matter as they navigate into their teenage years and beyond. When your daughter experiences her first crush, who would you like her to talk to about how she's feeling: her friends, someone in an online chat room, or you? If she's used to talking to you about what's going on in her life, chances are she will turn to you in this instance as well.

I was recently looking through a copy of a popular magazine for teenage girls and was shocked at the content of the pages that offered relationship advice, including sex topics. The target audience for this magazine is girls ages twelve to nineteen, but sometimes it reaches kids even younger. The values present there were not in line with Catholic moral teaching or Theology of the Body, not by a long shot. I can't imagine how uncomfortable it must be to have the sex talk with your son or daughter, but wouldn't you want that advice and accompanying values to come from you rather than from their friends or a popular magazine? A film that covers this topic, such as *A Walk to Remember* (although there are other issues in it as well), can be a good starting point for that all-important conversation you want to have with your children about the things they need to know in life.

But what if the kids run across a magazine or see a movie you may not approve of at their friend's house? The critical thinking skills they have developed by talking about media with you will enable them to either make the proper choices or to talk with you about the choice they did make. Who knows? Maybe your child will be able to explain to his friend what he liked about the movie and what he didn't like and why. He may become a "values ambassador" to his own friends through his use of critical thinking skills!

Third, values. When your child is baptized, part of the ritual, right before the profession of faith, is addressed directly to the parents and godparents: "On your part, you must make it your constant care to bring [the child] up in the practice of the faith. See that the divine life which God gives him/her is kept safe from poison of sin, to grow always stronger in his/her heart."[1] Thus, the Church appoints you the primary teachers from whom your kids will learn what being a Catholic Christian is all about. Your imagination will come up with millions of ways to do this.

One out of the millions is identifying and talking about the values present in movies. In these movies, you will run across good values like empathy, human dignity, and sacrifice. You will also see destructive values such as revenge, violence, and selfishness. Making connections between what happens to characters in the movie and your child's life will help her to see what the consequences of her choices in the face of a moral dilemma might be. Of course, you won't use those words when talking to her about it, but she'll grasp the concept. Then, with your guidance, she will begin to put these values into practice in her life.

Ultimately, the goal of practicing a family strategy for movies and other media, together with everything else you teach them, is that your children grow into faithful followers of Jesus Christ with the whole of their being.

Building the Strategy

Asking questions and giving answers. This is where communication happens. This is how people get to know one another. Questions force you to think and reflect. Building your family strategy for watching movies with your kids is not a step one, step two, step three process. It's thinking and reflecting on the questions posed below (and others you may come up with) and then answering them together in family dialogue and prayer. The answers to some questions will be harder to

---

1. Excerpt from the English translation of *Rite of Baptism for Children* © 1969, International Committee on English in the Liturgy, Inc. All rights reserved.

come to an agreement on than others. Putting into practice your agreed-upon answers might be easier in some instances than others. Hopefully, the answers to these questions will become part of your parental toolbox when it comes to addressing media in your family.

The strategy questions are arranged in three sections: Choosing the Movie, Approaching the Movie, and Questioning the Movie. Each section contains five questions. You can modify the questions so they are age-appropriate for your children. The answers to the questions may be very simple if your children are younger and more in-depth if they are a bit older. The important thing is to come to your answers together as a family. May the Lord guide you in this endeavor.

Questions to answer as a family regarding choosing movies

These questions are just a few of the myriad that could be asked about any movie, one's attitude toward movies, and what part movies will play in your family. I invite you to add your own questions and answers as the Holy Spirit inspires you. Use the blank lines for your own additional questions.

Choosing the Movie

1. What steps will we take in coming to a decision about what movies to watch?

_____

_____

_____

_____

2. How will our family's values (identified in Chapter Two) help us choose the movies we will watch?

_____

_____

_____

_____

3. How will we avail ourselves of reviews in deciding what movies to watch?

_____

_____

_____

_____

4. How will we use the ratings in deciding if a movie is appropriate or not?

_____

_____

_____

_____

5. If there are disagreements about choosing a movie, how will we talk over our disagreements? (If agreements cannot be made between parents and kids, how will parents explain their reasons to the kids?)

_____

_____

_____

_____

Additional questions

_____

_____

_____

_____

Approaching the movie

1. How will we use the media mindfulness circle to talk about the movie?

_____

_____

_____

_____

2. How will we confirm positive or address negative values in the movie?

_____

_____

_____

_____

3. How will we approach difficult issues portrayed in the movie?

_____

_____

_____

_____

_____

4. How can what was portrayed in this movie be brought into family prayer?

_____

_____

_____

_____

_____

5. How will we put the meaning made from the movie into practice in the way we live?

_____

_____

_____

_____

_____

Additional questions

_____

_____

_____

_____

Questioning the Movie

1. Use the questions on the media mindfulness circle.

_____

_____

_____

_____

2. Did any of the characters change during the movie? How? Was it for the better?

_____

_____

_____

_____

3. What would you do if you were that character? Why?

_____

_____

_____

_____

4. Were people respected in the movie? How? If not, why not?

_____

_____

_____

_____

5. Is there anything in the movie that bothered you? Let's talk about that.

_____

_____

_____

_____

Additional questions

_____

_____

_____

_____

When it comes to watching and making meaning from movies, there is no right or wrong, but only what the movie means to each person. Your understanding may be different from that of someone else, but no less valid. Your kids may understand the movie in a different way than you do, but their experience and opinion should also be considered valuable. This is what makes conversation around a movie so interesting and enriching. When people share their insights, they may come to understand something they never thought of before. Being able to see things from someone else's perspective and to respect that perspective is an invaluable skill. And with the commitment you and your family have just made together, all of you will be duly enriched by each other's presence, insight, and love.

SAINTS TO GUIDE US
Saint Clare of Assisi

Although this book is focusing on movies, television is often a part of a family's media experience. Sometimes you might even watch movies on TV. There is no official patron saint of movies or the film industry, but Saint Clare of Assisi is the patron saint of television.

Saint Clare was born into a family of nobility in Assisi, Italy, in 1193. She grew up with all that her family's wealth could buy even though she felt like something was missing. At a time in history when arranged marriages were common, Clare's position made her a desirable match, but she did not want to marry. Instead, she wanted to give her life to the Lord.

When Clare was eighteen, she met Saint Francis. He also came from a very wealthy family but had renounced his wealth, choosing to follow Jesus through a life of strict poverty. When Francis preached in Assisi, Clare listened and knew that she wanted to follow Francis, giving everything to God to live like Francis did, in complete reliance on God and the goodness of people. On Palm Sunday, 1212, against her parents' wishes but with permission of the local bishop, Clare went to Francis to begin the life she lived for the next forty years. In a symbol of dedication to God, he cut off her long hair and exchanged her fine clothes for a rough robe, similar to what the Friars wore, and a veil.

The group begun by Clare was called the "Poor Ladies." Francis turned the grounds of San Damiano Church over to Clare and the women who joined her. They depended totally on the generosity of others for their basic needs and dedicated their lives to prayer and labor. The "Poor Ladies" grew quickly and wherever the Franciscans went, so did Clare's nuns. Eventually, Clare's own sister, Agnes, and her widowed mother also joined her at the convent.

Following Saint Francis, Clare and her nuns lived the austere life they were called to by God. She established a "Rule" for the Poor Ladies and submitted it to the pope for approval. This, however, was slow in coming. The severity of the life the Sisters were living was unusual for the time, and Clare prayed that she would live to see papal acceptance of the rule for her community. God granted her wish. The "Rule" for the Poor Ladies was approved on August 9, 1253. Clare died two days later, on August 11, 1253, at the age of fifty-nine.

By that time, 150 communities of the Poor Clares, as they were called after her death, were spread out all over Europe. She was canonized a saint two years later.

In 1958, Pope Pius XII named Saint Clare the patron saint of television. It seems a little funny that someone who lived and died way before the television was invented could be considered its patron saint, but in God's divine plan, the saints can intercede for us in ways we might not imagine! An incident in Saint Clare's life explains the pope's choice of her as patron saint of television. On the night of Christmas, 1252, Saint Clare was too ill to attend Mass in honor of Jesus's birth, but God gave her the grace to be able to see the Mass from her cell, miraculously displayed on the cell's wall! Saint Clare of Assisi, pray for us.

Chapter Six

Family Activities

Up until now, we have focused on understanding the media world in which we live, the values present in it, and how to ask questions of media, specifically movies, to arrive at meaning. You and your family have worked on a plan to integrate movie watching and conversation into your family's fun time to make some of it sacred time as well. With the brief look at some techniques moviemakers use, Chapter Three took a small step into explaining what goes into making a film. With this chapter, media production becomes a reality. What better way to learn what goes into media than to do it yourself? Production has always been a part of formal media studies because in the process of actually making a media production, you understand better the choices and decisions that go into the movies we watch.

For example, when I studied media literacy, four other students and I had to put together a news story of some kind. We chose to do a feature on writer's block. Using a camera from the school, we shot interviews of students, shot filler images called *B-roll*, recorded voice-over (a narrator talking over images), and introduced and finished the segment. It was a fun project, but the five of us came to realize that a whole lot of hard work goes into a news story that can take only one or two minutes (sometimes even less) of air time. We had to choose which interviews and parts of interviews to include in our segment. We had to write the script for the voice-over and even had to do some last minute interviews because our earlier ones had sound problems. Then we edited the segment together, with some help, and added some music to the end credits. It definitely was not a CNN production, but we learned a lot from the experience.

The activities in this chapter are fun ways to learn even more about how a media text is put together. With this kind of experience, you and your kids will better be able to understand the choices made by those who produce the media you experience. You don't need a lot of technical know-how to do these activities, but access to a computer will be necessary for some of them. Who knows? Maybe your kids already know how to do some of this stuff and can teach you!

Make Your Own Storyboard

The first step in making a movie is to have a story written out in the form of a script detailing what your characters will say and do. From the script, a storyboard, a set of drawings that show the visual details of the movie, is made. This shows who will be in each shot and what camera angle will be used. Sometimes you find arrows indicating that a character is moving. The purpose is to help you visualize your film before you start filming.

You don't have to be an artist to make a storyboard. Stick figures will do, but you can make your storyboard as fancy as you want. Here's an example drawn by me.

① Alexa looking through scrunchie box
Intro as Voice over
camera: medium range.

② Putting more scrunchies in hair & arm
Voice over continues
camera: zoom in

③ Alexa looks happily in the mirror
voice over continues
Camera: medium close-up

④ Paul looks through the door
Bul: Are those ponytail holders or bracelets?
camera: medium range

⑤ Alexa turns to look at Paul, grinning
Alexa: Both!
Camera: close-up on Alexa

What You Will Need

○ Some paper, pencil, and an eraser

○ Storyboard template

What to Do

○ Trace the storyboard template onto a sheet of paper or you can download and print one out from www.xinsight.ca/tools/storyboard.html. I can't vouch for any other content on this Web site, but they have a nice storyboard template. (Our storyboard template can be found on the Media Mindfulness tab at www.JClubCatholic.org.)

○ Think of a story that would make a good movie such as a favorite storybook or story from the Gospel, or make up your own.

○ Draw what it would look like on your storyboard sheets, including instructions such as camera angle and movement.

Frame It!

The camera is one of the main tools used by a moviemaker. There is no movie unless something has been filmed (unless, of course, the movie is totally computer generated). This activity lets you be the camera person, framing shots.

What You Will Need

○ A piece of paper and the diagram of a camera (the diagram can be found on the Media Mindfulness tab at www.JClubCatholic.org OR

○ digital camera and computer with PowerPoint presentation graphics program, if desired

What to Do

○ If you are using paper, trace the camera onto a blank sheet and cut along the dotted lines for your lens.

○ Choose a subject for your photos. It could be anything, a person, tree, or the kitchen sink!

○ Use the screen of the camera (or the hole in your paper camera) to frame your photo.

○ Notice how as you move the camera different things come into focus. Look at your subject from different angles. If you have a digital camera, take pictures of your subject from a variety of angles: close-up, medium range, long range, from above, from below.

○ If your digital camera also shoots video, make a short video of your subject. Experiment with zooming in and out and panning.

○ Think about these questions:

What happens when the angle changes?

How do the different angles change the look of the photos?

Did you choose to leave something out of the picture? Why?

○ If you wish, when finished taking your pictures, load them into the computer and make a PowerPoint presentation explaining each photo, its angle, and why you chose to do it a certain way. Show the presentation to your family or friends and talk about what you learned from the experience.

Make Your Own Movie

Making a movie is a big undertaking. The studios making the movies you see in the theater collaborate with many people to make a movie, often spending millions of dollars in the process. That's not exactly the kind of movie I'm suggesting here. Just something simple.

If you've already done the above activities, they are steps in making your own movie. You can make your storyboard into a movie or even the pictures you took in the Frame It activity.

What You Will Need

○ Digital camera that takes video OR

○ Any type of video camera

○ Mac computer with the iMovie application, or PC with Windows Movie Maker

What to Do

○ Take the video footage you need for your story or you can also use still photographs. Assign roles: who will be the actor, the director, the cinematographer (camera person), the editor?

○ Edit your movie using iMovie software (for a Mac computer) or Windows Movie Maker (for a PC) and share it with your family and friends.

○   During the process think of these things:

>   Why did you choose the story you did?

>   What kinds of decisions were needed as you made your movie? Why did you make those choices?

>   Did you have technical difficulties? Were they easy to solve or did you have to get some help? Movie making takes a lot of people with specific areas of expertise.

Make Your Own Podcast

Movies and television are more popular today than radio, yet many people utilize radio for a number of reasons. They listen to music, traffic reports, sports broadcasts, and news. The Internet has made access to almost any radio station possible no matter where you are. I enjoy listening to classical music while I work, and the best classical radio station I know is in Boston, even though I live in Los Angeles. I can play Boston's radio station on my computer and listen while I work.

Besides music, audio technology gives people the opportunity for their own voices to be heard through podcasting. Anyone with a computer and a microphone (Mac computers have microphones built in) can produce a podcast and post it on the Internet for anyone to download and hear. Parents, make sure the kids follow your rules regarding Internet use.

What You Will Need

○   Computer and microphone (some computers have microphones built in)

○   Software to put the podcast together. Garage Band audio editing software comes with the Mac computer. For PC, Audacity is a simple audio editing program that can be downloaded free from www.audacity.sourceforge.net. Audacity also works on the Mac computer, and some believe it is easier to use than Garage Band.

○ Web server to post your podcast. There are a number of Web sites that host podcasts, the most popular being the iTunes application. You can also try www.podbean.com. If you want your podcast to stay private and not be available to everyone, there are settings on Podbean allowing only those you invite to listen to your podcast.

What to Do

○ You will need an idea. What would you like to say to the world? You can write a script if you want, but you can also just talk if you so choose.

○ Record your podcast and transfer the file into your editing software.

○ Edit your podcast. If you wish you can put music under your words. Some editing programs provide non-copyrighted public performance music you can use. If your program does not have any, there are a number of Web sites that have free downloadable music. Just search for "free podcast music," and a number of Web sites will come up. You don't want to get into any copyright issues when doing your podcast. Post your podcast on a server and tell your family and friends about it so they can download and listen.

A note to parents: If you and your children produce anything with the intention of putting it online, make sure that there is no personal information about the child in the production. Your children's online safety is paramount. For tips on Internet safety, see suggestions at www.safekids.com.

Make a Family Blog

Blogging is another way to get your opinions and perspectives out to many people. A blog is a special Web site that is just for you. It's a place where you can post family news and even upload pictures of family events such as birthday parties. A blog is a way to get your news out without having to communicate individually with each person.

A blog enables you to have your own Web address, and this can be made private with access only to those you allow to have it. For example, although my blog is public and not private, I can easily make it private and give out the Web address only to people I want to have access. My blog address is www.sisterhosea.wordpress.com.

What You Will Need

○ Computer with Internet access

What to Do

○ Decide if this will be a blog for just one person or the whole family. Also decide what you will and will not post on the blog. Have a set of rules in place for everyone to follow. See www.safekids.com for tips on Internet safety for children.

○ Choose a blogging Web site. I recommend www.wordpress.com because it is very user-friendly and easy to learn. Another one is www.blogger.com.

○ Follow the instructions on the Web site for setting up a blog. Once you are set up and have done your first post, let those you choose know your Web address, so they can look at your blog. Suggest that they subscribe to your blog so that they will be notified when you make a new post.

○ Don't forget to post often. If you don't post for a long time, people won't come back to read your blog. I try to post at least once a week, but I know people who post every day.

A variation on starting a blog would be to begin a blog of the media your family experiences. Write down the name of the movie or television show you watched, what family members said about it when you discussed it, and what kind of values or meaning was gleaned from the experience. This blog will be fun to share with your extended family or with the families of your friends.

Have Your Own Film Festival

You might like to get together as a family, or invite some friends over for a fun time watching movies. You can hold your own in-house film festival. Choose some movies according to a theme and prepare a few points to discuss afterwards. Don't forget the popcorn!

My colleague, Sr. Rose Pacatte, FSP, has authored a little booklet on how to run an in-house film festival. It can be downloaded for free from the JClub Web site for children: www.jclubcatholic.org/downloads/pt_media/FilmFestivalGuide.pdf.

Chapter Seven

Some Resources to Get You Started

Now that you have developed your family strategy for watching movies with your kids, here are a few additional resources to help you on your journey. I hope you find them useful.

Sample Film Guides

In this section, I've listed ten children's films. Some are classics, some are more recent, and one is a foreign-language film. Most of these films are readily available wherever movies are sold or rented. *Children of Heaven,* an Iranian film, is available for rental through Netflix. As conversation starters, I have provided a few questions based on each film. As you watch movies with the kids, I'm sure you will come up with questions and insights of your own to talk about with them.

Bridge to Terabithia (2007)

1. Talk about what family life was like in Jess Aarons's house.

2. Two boys in Jess's class made fun of him for his shoes, and for other things as well. How would you feel if you were being made fun of like Jess was? How do you respond to a bully?

3. Leslie teaches Jess to use his imagination, and they have a great time in Terabithia, their magical kingdom. What part does imagination play in your life?

4. Leslie reaches out to Janice Avery when she's upset, and Janice becomes her friend, defending her and Jess from the bullies. Is it easy to be nice to those who have not been nice to you?

5. How does Jess deal with Leslie's death? What did you think about him building the bridge and taking May Belle with him to Terabithia? What would you have done if you were Jess?

Children of Heaven (1997)

A note about foreign-language films: While their films don't often make it to our movie theaters, the film industry is thriving in some other countries of the world, and their cinematic offerings are not to be ignored. Often times, foreign films are much deeper and more thought-provoking than their North American counterparts. *Children of Heaven*, made in Iran, is a great place to start introducing your children to foreign film. Try not to be intimidated by the subtitles. They do take some getting used to.

1. Was it Ali's fault that Zahra's shoes got lost? Why do you think he didn't want to tell his mom or dad about it? What would you have done?
2. How did Ali and Zahra show their love for each other? How do you show love for your family?
3. Ali and Zahra's family is poor, but they still show generosity to their neighbors. How do you share what you have with others?
4. Ali's dad finds work as a gardener and is able to buy some things his family needs. Instead of asking for something for himself, Ali asks his dad to buy Zahra a new pair of shoes. What would you have done in Ali's place? How do you think it made Ali's dad feel to be able to provide for his family?
5. What pushes Ali to run the race? Why is he so disappointed that he didn't come in third? How would you feel?

E.T.: The Extra-Terrestrial (1982)

1. E.T. just wanted to get home. What does "home" mean to you?
2. Why do you think Elliott began to share E.T.'s feelings?

3. E.T. dies, so Elliott can live. Then he comes back to life. Does this remind you of the story of Jesus's death and resurrection?

4. What does this movie say about the way we treat those who are different from us?

5. E.T. tells Elliott, "I'll be right here." Jesus also promised that he would be with us until the end of time (Mt 28:20). Why is it important to know we are not alone?

Hannah Montana: The Movie (2009)

1. What do you really know about the celebrities you admire? Do the things they do in their lives make them good role models? Why or why not?

2. The people of Crowley's Corner seem to care for each other. What does community mean to you?

3. Travis tells Miley, "Life's a climb, but the view's great." What does this mean? What is Miley's climb? What is yours?

4. What does this movie say about honesty and telling the truth?

5. If you were in Miley Stewart's place, would you choose being Miley or being Hannah? Why?

Horton Hears a Who! (2008)

1. Kangaroo tells Horton that if you can't see or hear or feel something, it doesn't exist. Is this true? Give an example of something that you can't see or hear or feel that does exist.

2. Horton believed what the Mayor of Whoville said about people living on the speck, but none of the other jungle creatures did. Is it easy to trust that what other people say is the truth? How do you show your friends that you trust what they say?

3. When the jungle animals rope and cage Horton, it's like what happened to Jesus. What does it feel like when others make fun

of you? Have you ever said anything hurtful to someone else? Did they forgive you?

4. Horton says, "A person's a person no matter how small." What does this mean to you?

5. The Whos needed every voice in order to be heard, even Jojo's. Talk about how each person is important no matter how unimportant they may seem.

The Incredibles (2004)

1. Why did the people not want to have the "Supers" defending them anymore? Were the Supers doing something wrong? How would you feel if people did not appreciate what you were doing for them?

2. Why was it hard for Dash and Violet to hide their powers? Is it hard for you to hide your talents? Why or why not?

3. Mr. Incredible tells Buddy to go home. How would you feel if that happened to you? Was Mr. Incredible right in telling him to go away or was Mr. Incredible trying to protect Buddy?

4. When Mr. Incredible threatened Mirage to get to Syndrome, he did not have the heart to harm her. Later when talking to Syndrome, Mirage says, "He is not weak. Valuing life is not weakness." What does this mean to you?

5. How would you describe the family life of the Incredibles throughout the movie? Were they a happy, loving family? Why or why not? How would you describe your family?

Nim's Island (2008)

1. The three main characters in the film (Nim, Jack, Alexandra) all showed courage. How? Does courage play any part in your daily life? Why or why not?

2. Although Nim and her father live alone on the island, Nim has a community of friends in the animals. Who (or what) are the important communities in your life?

3. Why were the passengers of the buccaneer ship a threat to Nim and the island? What does this have to say about our treatment of the earth and about commercialization?

4. What was it that helped Alexandra to overcome her fears and respond to Nim's messages? How do you overcome the fears you have?

5. Nim's imagination was very active, encouraged by the Alex Rover novels. Does imagination enrich you? Why or why not?

Robots (2005)

1. What do you think of Mr. Big Weld's motto: "You can shine no matter what you're made of"? What does it mean to you?

2. Why does Rodney admire Mr. Big Weld? How has he learned values from his mom and dad?

3. When Ratchet takes over Big Weld Industries, he changes the motto to: "Why be you, when you can be new." How is this different from Mr. Big Weld's motto? What does it mean to you?

4. Mr. Big Weld tells Rodney about the takeover of his company by Ratchet. He says, "For me, it was about making life better, for Ratchet it's about making money." Which one seems more important to you? Why?

5. Piper tells the hardware store robot, "We are not junk, we are not scrap, and we will not be treated this way." Why were the outmodes treated badly? Would you like it if you were treated like that? Is there anything you should change about how you treat others?

To Kill a Mockingbird (1962)

1. Atticus tells Scout about empathy: "You never really understand a person until you consider things from his point of view, climb into his skin and walk around in it." Talk about what this means for you.
2. Because Atticus takes Tom Robinson's case, the kids begin to be bullied at school. Both Jem and Scout get into fights over it. Have you ever been ridiculed for doing the right thing? How does it feel?
3. Atticus tells Jem: "There's lots of ugly things in this world, son. I wish I could keep them all away from you. That's never possible." What kind of ugly things do you think Atticus was talking about? Talk as a family about the ugly things you see in the world.
4. The kids spend a lot of time talking about "Boo" Radley, the mysterious man who lives down the street. They make dares to go up and touch his door. What are the kids afraid of? How does "Boo" show that he cares about them? It was "Boo" who saved Jem at the end of the movie. Talk about how Scout reaches out to him and becomes his friend.
5. In the courtroom after the verdict is delivered, all the African Americans remain in the courthouse, standing in respect for Atticus. What does this scene tell you about respect, honor, and honorable behavior?

The Wizard of Oz (1939)

1. When Dorothy wanted to go home, she was told to journey along the Yellow Brick Road. What does this path symbolize? What is your Yellow Brick Road? What friends do you have to help you along the way?

2. The Scarecrow wants a brain. How did he prove he already had a brain even before the Wizard gave him a diploma?

3. When the three friends went off the Yellow Brick Road into the poppies, what happened? Then they asked for help. How is this like prayer? Who do you ask for help when you pray?

4. When the Tin Man received his heart, the Wizard tells him that what is important is how much he is loved by others. What does this mean? How do you show others that you love them? What does it feel like to be loved by others?

5. Before Dorothy can go home, she is asked what she learned. What did you learn from this movie?

Movies and Themes

The list below takes some common values and Christian themes and lists movies that deal with those themes. The list is in no way comprehensive. My hope is that this list will help you make some connections between movies and Christian themes or values. You can add to the list movies you think fit the various categories.

Family

An American Tail

Wide Awake

The Incredibles

Finding Neverland

Charlie and the Chocolate Factory

Imagine That

Corrina, Corrina

Yours, Mine and Ours

Spy Kids

Dreamer
E.T.: The Extra-Terrestrial
Cheaper By the Dozen
Fly Away Home
Nanny McPhee

Hope

An American Tail
August Rush
Pinocchio
Dreamer
Nim's Island
Fly Away Home

Service

Up

Friendship

Up
Finding Neverland
Babe
The Mighty
The *Harry Potter* film series

Community

The Land Before Time
Charlotte's Web
Over the Hedge
Toy Story
The Thief Lord

Transformation

Over the Hedge

Finding Neverland

Nanny McPhee

The Ant Bully

Horton Hears a Who!

Ratatouille

Night at the Museum

Remember the Titans

Mean Girls

Because of Winn-Dixie

The Wizard of Oz

E.T.: The Extra-Terrestrial

Cheaper By the Dozen

Hannah Montana: The Movie

Kindness

Nanny McPhee

Babe

Charlie and the Chocolate Factory

Monsters, Inc.

Acceptance

Racing Stripes

The Secret Garden

The Incredibles

Robots

Remember the Titans

Hannah Montana: The Movie

Faith

Wide Awake

Toy Story

Arthur & The Invisibles

Corrina, Corrina

The Chronicles of Narnia: Prince Caspian

The Mighty

Nim's Island

Millions

Simon Birch

Sacrifice

Charlie and the Chocolate Factory

Horton Hears a Who!

The Chronicles of Narnia:
    The Lion, the Witch, and the Wardrobe

The Lion King

The *Harry Potter* film series

E.T.: The Extra-Terrestrial

Simon Birch

Reconciliation

Raise Your Voice

The Chronicles of Narnia:
    The Lion, the Witch, and the Wardrobe

Love

August Rush

Night at the Museum

Snow Dogs

The Lion King

Wizard of Oz

Cheaper By the Dozen

Commitment

Yours, Mine and Ours

The Chronicles of Narnia: Prince Caspian

The Karate Kid

The *Harry Potter* film series

Generosity

The Thief Lord

Millions

Respect

The Indian in the Cupboard

To Kill a Mockingbird

Other Resources

Online Resources

A good online search for a film review of any movie will yield a bunch of options. Which ones do you choose to look at? Here are some Web sites I have found helpful in the past. Also, don't forget to check your local newspaper for film reviews. I know the *Los Angeles Times* (www.latimes.com/entertainment/news/movies) has a great review section, as does the *New York Times* (www.movies.nytimes. com/ref/movies/reviews). In Canada, the *Toronto Star* (www.thestar. com/entertainment/movies) also has good movie coverage.

Center for Media Literacy— www.medialit.org

Many resources are available for parents and teachers as well as archived articles from the *Media & Values* magazine.

Commonsense Media— www.commonsensemedia.org

This is a site specifically for parents with reviews and ratings for movies, TV shows, Web sites, video games, etc. A unique feature is the site's suggestions about the age-appropriateness of the media they review. Parents and kids can also post reviews. They also provide many articles about media-related topics.

Hollywood Jesus— www.hollywoodjesus.com

Movie reviews from a Christian perspective.

Internet Movie Database— www.imdb.com

On this site you can find just about any movie ever made. There are many reviews and other information as well.

Media Literacy Clearinghouse—
www.frankbaker.com

Resources to better understand media literacy. This site is designed for teachers, but parents will also find a wealth of great information.

Safe Kids—
www.safekids.com

Internet safety for parents and kids.

Understand Media—
www.understandmedia.com

This site offers media literacy information for teachers and parents. It emphasizes using technology to teach and learn. You might find help here for some of the activities in Chapter Six.

United States Conference of Catholic Bishops' Office for Film and Broadcasting—
www.usccb.org/movies

Film reviews and a rating system. The ratings used by this site are different than your average MPAA ratings. Click on "criteria" for a detailed explanation of the classifications used.

Virtus Online—
www.virtus.org

This site contains resource articles regarding the safety of children. You can also get details on the various programs they offer for parish volunteers, catechists, and anyone doing ministry with children.

Visual Parables— www.visualparables.net

This is a subscription site that reviews films from a Christian perspective, linking Scripture to film and making suggestions for using film examples in sermons.

Wing Clips— www.wingclips.com

This site features free, downloadable clips from popular Hollywood films. Enter a theme, such as forgiveness, into the search area and a whole list of suggested clips come up.

Ratings Sites

As mentioned in Chapter Four, here are the sites that explain the most common rating systems in the United States and Canada.

Motion Picture Association of America—www.mpaa.org

Canadian Film Classification Offices

British Columbia—www.bcfilmclass.com
Alberta—www.albertafilmratings.ca
Saskatchewan—uses the ratings from British Columbia
Manitoba—www.gov.mb.ca/chc/mfcb
Ontario—www.ofrb.gov.on.ca
Quebec—www.rcq.qc.ca/mult/home.asp?lng=en
Maritimes—www.gov.ns.ca/lwd/agd/film

Of the Territories, the Yukon uses British Columbia ratings, and Nunavut and the Northwest Territories use Alberta ratings.

Helpful Books

Baker, Frank. *Coming Distractions: Questioning the Movies.* Mankato, MN: Capstone Press, 2007.

Teaches elementary school students how to question movies.

Hailer, Gretchen, and Rose Pacatte. *Media Mindfulness: Educating Teens about Faith and Media.* Winona, MN: Saint Mary's Press, 2007.

A resource for high school teachers on integrating faith and media. Covers the various media such as radio, television, movies, advertising as well as popular culture and theology of communication.

————. *Our Media World: Teaching Kids K–8 About Faith and Media.* Boston, MA: Pauline Books & Media, 2010.

Lesson plans for kindergarten through eighth grade on media literacy. It has great activities and resources for teachers and parents.

Keaton, Mary Margaret. *Imagining Faith with Kids: Unearthing Seeds of the Gospel in Children's Stories from Peter Rabbit to Harry Potter.* Boston, MA: Pauline Books & Media, 2005.

Looks at classic and contemporary children's stories from a Gospel perspective.

United States Conference of Catholic Bishops. *The National Directory for Catechesis.* Washington, DC: USCCB Publishing, 2005.

Acknowledgments

Grateful acknowledgment is made to the Intercollegiate Studies Institute for permission to use a quote from Vigen Guroian's article "Awakening the Moral Imagination: Teaching Virtues Through Fairy Tales" from the Fall 1996 *Intercollegiate Review*. © All rights reserved.

Audacity® software is copyright © 1999–2010 Audacity Team. The name Audacity® is a registered trademark of Dominic Mazzoni.

This book makes reference to various Disney copyrighted characters, trademarks, marks, and registered marks owned by The Walt Disney Company and Disney Enterprises, Inc.

Mac, iMovie, and iTunes are trademarks of Apple Inc., registered in the United States and other countries.

Windows and PowerPoint are registered trademarks of Microsoft Corporation in the United States and other countries.

Supernanny is a registered trademark of Ricochet Productions Limited.

BOOKS & MEDIA

A mission of the Daughters of St. Paul

As apostles of Jesus Christ, evangelizing today's world:

We are CALLED to holiness
by God's living Word and Eucharist.

We COMMUNICATE the Gospel message
through our lives and through all
available forms of media.

We SERVE the Church
by responding to the hopes and needs
of all people with the Word of God,
in the spirit of St. Paul.

For more information visit our website: www.pauline.org.